The 2nd Amendment
A well regulated militia, being necessary to the security of a free state, the right of the people to keep and bear arms, shall not be infringed.
S.R.C. Combatives
Get Real
Adams Karate

When it's Least Expected You're Elected!

Watch You're Six

Train, train, and train....

DISCLAIMER

Note: This publication contains opinions and ideas of its author. It is attended to provide helpful and informative material on the subject matter covered. The author and publisher specifically disclaim and responsibility for any liability, loss, or risk, personal or otherwise, which is incurred consequently, directly, or indirectly, of the use and application of any of the contents of this book.

Disclaimer: Please note that the publisher and author of the book are NOT RESPONSIBLE in any matter whatsoever for any injury that may result from practicing the techniques and/or following instructions given within. Martial Arts training can be dangerous - both to you and to others - if not practiced safely. If you are in doubt as to how to proceed or whether your practice is safe, consult with a trained martial Arts teacher before begging,

Super "T" Karate Inc. Terry Gay and Lloyd D. Adams or any other person included on or associated with this book or website / video makes no representation, warranty, or guarantee that the techniques described or illustrated in this book / video will be safe and effective in a self-defense situation or otherwise.

It is essential that before doing any physical activities you should first consult a physician.

THIS BOOK IS FOR REFERENCE PURPOSE ONLY

Get Real

And Be

Be Safe

Acknowledgments

The creation of this book is due to the influence and support over my years in the martial arts with many great people.

I would like to thank my Great Friend and Highest-Ranking Black Belt Student Shihan Lloyd D. Adams for his contribution to this book with the photography. My children Nathan, Ryan, and Leah for their help in this book.

Terry Gay

DEDICATION

This Book is Dedicated with Love and Honor to the Memory of My Son TJ Gay.

FOREWORD

Welcome to the Super T Tactical Defense Handbook.
This book is intended to introduce you to the fundamentals of the
Super T Tactical Defense System.

When under stress an individual will fall back upon those fundamentals that are
conditioned to muscle memory. This conditioning comes from many repetitions
of doing the movements over and over.
Super T Tactical Defense is a Division of the Super T Karate System.

- Seminars

- Workshops

- Lectures

- Private Lessons

Contact Terry at (616) 364-5111

www.supertkarate.com

Table of Contents

Terry Gay is the founder of Super T Karate / Tactical Defense, a school that prides itself on teaching practical self-defense, hand-to-hand combat, edged weapons training, and firearm training.

Terry Gay has been teaching martial arts for over 40+ years. Along with his martial art training, he loves to share his knowledge of firearm tactics, knife tactics, and personal protection.

Terry regularly trains and participates in professional development courses to improve and increase his skills, so that he may offer a better learning experience for his students and clients. Terry teaches full-time from his Martial Arts school, Super T Karate in Grand Rapids Michigan. He is a qualified handler of firearms, and instructor of proper firearm and knife handling, He teaches courses from fundamentals all the way to advanced tactical handgun training for real world self-defense.

Training:

- 8th Degree Black Belt
- 46+ Years Martial Arts Experience
- P.A.K.A. World Kickboxing Champion
- Certified Cage Combat MMA Referee
- ISCF Certified MMA Referee
- ISCF Certified MMA Judge
- International Hall of Fame Member
- NRA Certified Firearms Instructor
- USCCA Certified Firearms Instructor
- SRC Defensive Knife Instructor
- Former Professional Boxer & Kickboxing
- CQT Carbine 1 & 2
- Personal Protection Security
- Security Guard / Bouncer
- Defensive Tactics Instructor
- UDEMY Defensive Handgun
- Ranger Tactical Handgun
- NTL Affiliate Instructor
- Certified, Member of the Association of Defensive Shooting Instructors
- Bravery Award Branch County Sheriff Dept
- C.R.A.V.A.T - Civilian Response to Active Violence and Trauma Training
- 100+ Hours Force on Force Training
- KMMA USA Krav Maga Martial Arts Tactical Weapons Instructor
- CQT Handgun 1 & 2
- CQT Low Light
- Gideon Training Services Inc. Defensive Handgun
- A3 Fighting from The Vehicle
- RSO Range Safety Officer
- CC Vehicle Firearm Tactics
- NLT Handgun Gripe Development
- Shooter Technology Group Ultimate Dry Fire Training Program
- CC Complete Home Defense - Tactics for Defending Your Castle
- Dave Spaulding Handgun Combatives

Super T Family

Shihan Lloyd Adams	**Master Terry Gay**
Adams Karate	Super T Karate
www.adamskaratefitness.com	www.supertkarate.com

EDC / Everyday Carry:

Refers to items that are carried on a consistent basis to assist in dealing with normal everyday needs of modern society, including possible emergency self-defense situations.

 Wear a strong weight bearing belt being a leather or tactical style.

 Reliable cell phone with 911 programmed in it.

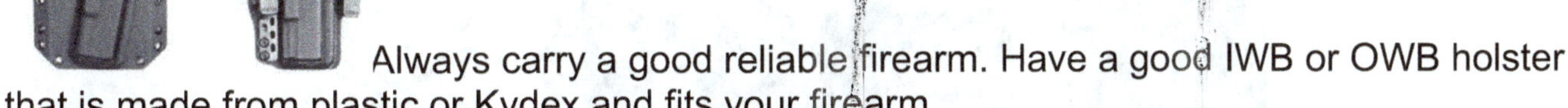

 Always carry a good reliable firearm. Have a good IWB or OWB holster that is made from plastic or Kydex and fits your firearm.

 Extra magazine and an easily accessible pouch.

 Bright reliable Flashlight with a thumb button.

 Good reliable tourniquet either a CAT, SOFTT-W tourniquet.

Sharp reliable knife.

EDC Knives

Knives can be hidden very easy and accessed fast.

EDC Knives

S.R.C. Combatives
Neck Knife
SOG Snarl
Recon 1
FOX Karambit
Ankle Knife

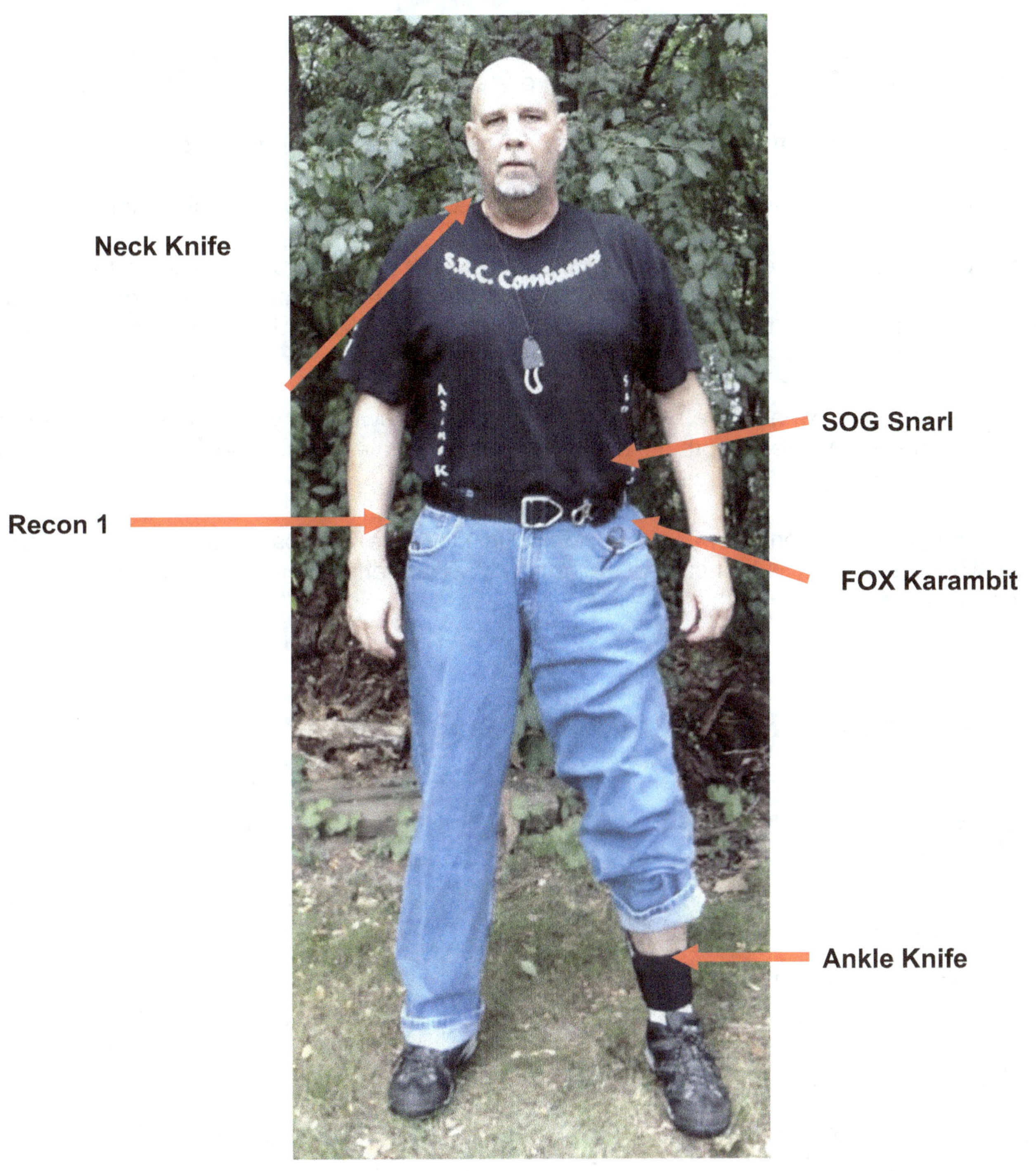

Situational Awareness!

Practice good Situational Awareness! Look around, keep your head on swivel and look for pre-incident indicators. There are usually warning or danger signs that precede an attack.

Do you know what they are, and have you honed your abilities to see these signs?

Remember and practice Colonel Jeff Cooper's Color Code system of Mental Readiness.

Maintain Distance or Space between you and a potential threat. If not distance, find an obstacle or barrier to get behind if needed. Most trainers describe the reactionary gap as 6 feet or more. Always keep your body bladed with your strong side to the back and your hands in a interview position.

Always look for an Escape Route. Again, put you head on swivel, if you can find an opening to disengage, take it. There is nothing wrong with running away and seeking a better tactical position.

Simple enough: Situational Awareness, Maintain Distance or Space, and look for Escape Routes. These are all skills that can be trained daily. Train effectively and often and remember to always pay attention!

Coopers Color Code:

White	Unprepared and unready to take action.
Yellow	Prepared, alert & relaxed. Good situational awareness.
Orange	Alert to probable danger. Ready to take action.
Red	Action Mode. Focused on the emergency at hand.
Black	Panic. Breakdown of physical & mental performance.

Threat Management:

- **Threat Identification-**

* Situation

    * OODA Loop (Observe, Orientate, Decide, Act)

    * Best way out of a situation is not to get in one

    * Hands / Weapon – Always Look

    * Gauge intent

    * Priority of Threat-

        * Distance

        * Danger Level

        * Fist available

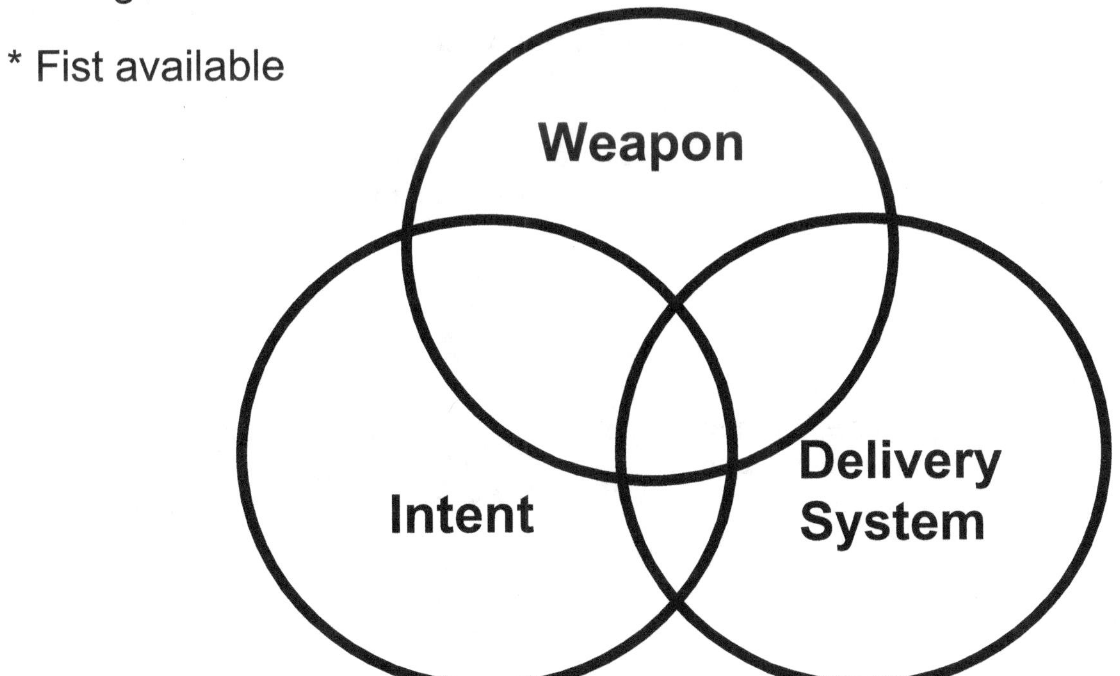

The Four - Pillars of Survival:

#1 Proper Mindset:____
____
____
____

#2 Situational Awareness: _____________________________________
____
____
____

#3 Skill Proficiency:____
____
____
____

#4 Physical Fitness____
____
____
____

Colonel John Boyd OODA Loop:

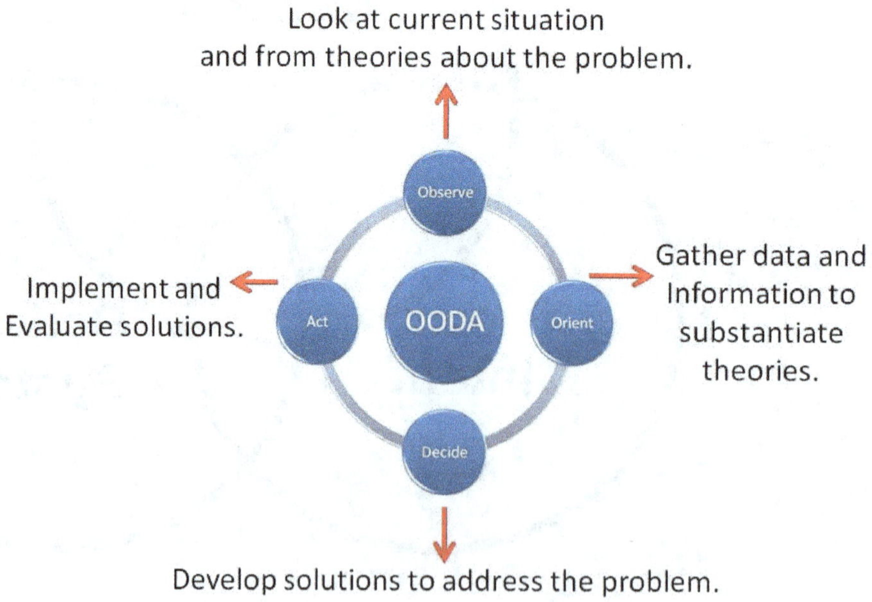

Super T EDC
Tactical Handgun

Firearms Safety Rules:

<u>FIREARMS</u> - Are Always Loaded.
<u>ALWAYS</u> - Keep Your Finger OFF the Trigger Until Ready to Shoot.
<u>ALWAYS</u> - Never Point Your Muzzle at Anything You Are Not Willing to Destroy.
<u>ALWAYS</u> - Know Your Target AND What's Beyond it.

NO Live Ammo in Classrooms

- All firearms need to have their slide locked back
- All magazines should be on the table next to the firearm unloaded.
- Snap caps/dummy rounds should be laid out on the table.
- All students need to empty their pockets and place all items on the table.
- All students will be searched and padded down to make sure there is **NO live ammo**.
- Anytime a student leaves the sterile area they will be searched again.

RANGE PROTOCAL:

- **NO** student will load their Firearm until given the command to do so.
- **NO** magazines to be loaded until they get the command to do so.
- Everyone **MUST** Have Eyes and Ears on before any shooting is started.
- Students that are not shooting must be always back in safe zone.
- Never bend down to pick up anything that has dropped until the instructor gives the Line is Safe command.
- Shooting needs to always be even.

- ## RANGE COMMANDS:
  Condition 1 – Load and make the Firearm Hot – Ready to Fire,
- **Condition 4** – Slide is locked back, and magazine is in your support hand.
  Threat / Fight / Gun – Command to start firing.
- **Line is Safe** – You can now pick up anything that has been dropped.

Ready Grips:

3rd eye

Sul

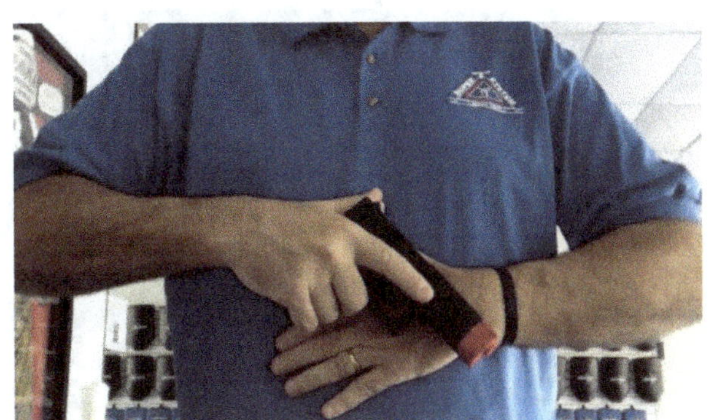

RIP

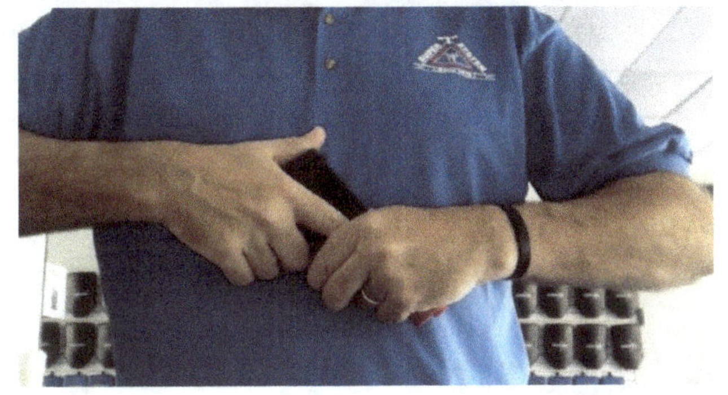

High Ready

Notes:

____

____

____

____

____

____

____

____

____

Shooting Stances:

Isosceles

Weaver

Combat / Fighting

Gripping Your Handgun:

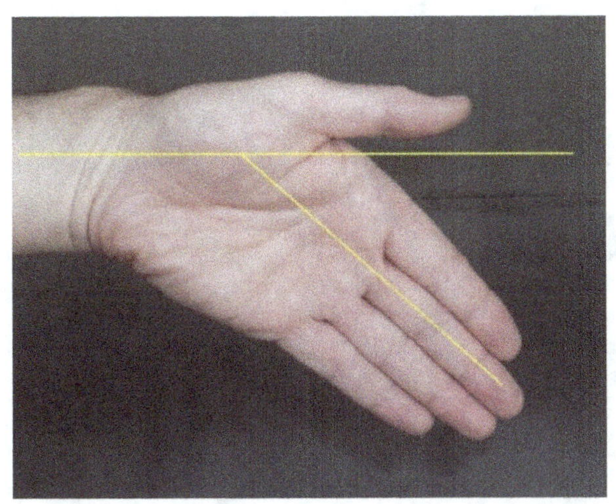

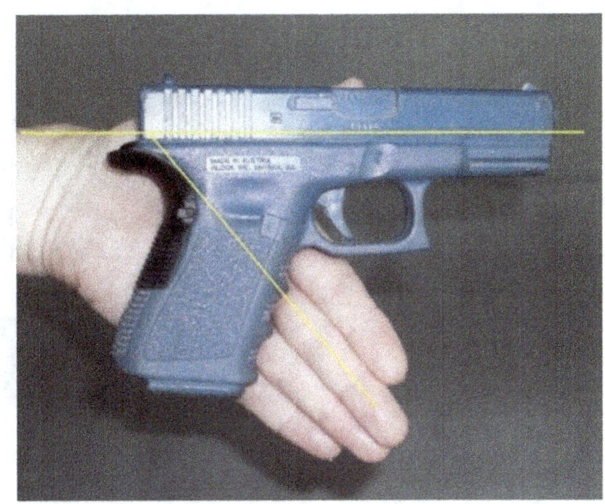

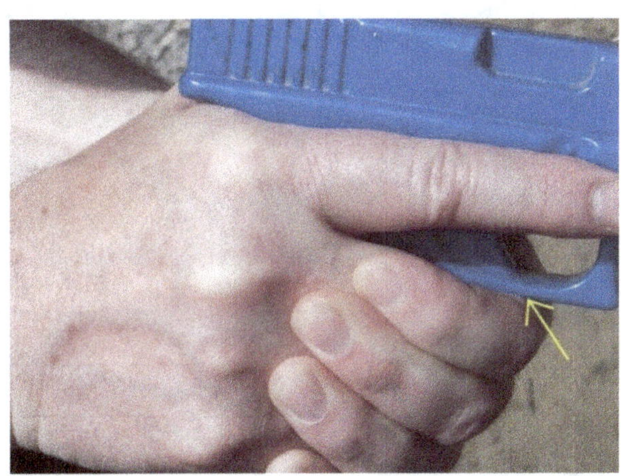

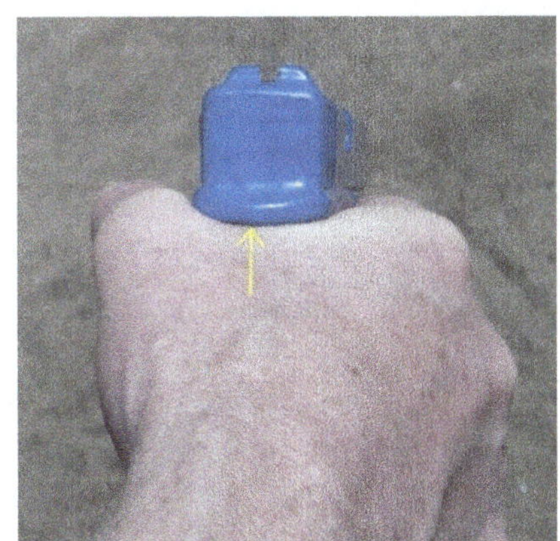

Sight Picture:

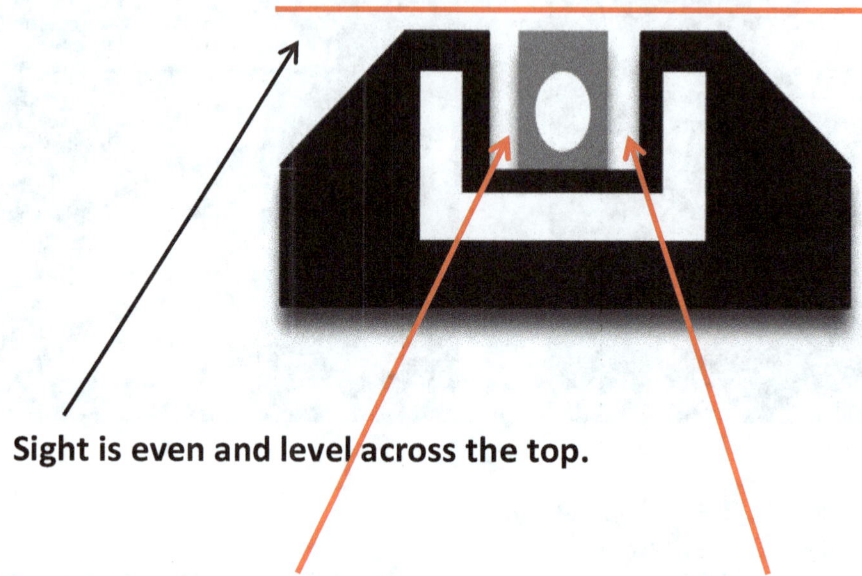

Notes:

____

____

____

____

____

____

____

____

____

____

____

____

Trigger Control:

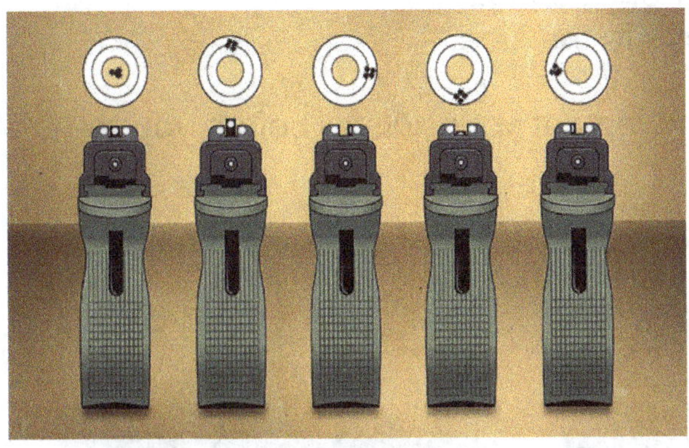

Examples of sight aliment

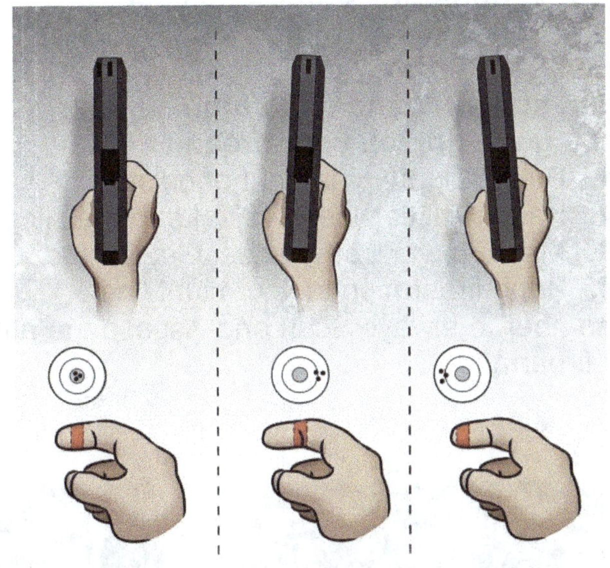

Examples of finger placement.

Notes:

____
____
____
____
____
____
____
____
____
____
____
____
____

Drawing Your Handgun:

<u>**Drawing:**</u>
-- Slow is Smooth -- Smooth is Fast

4- Step Draw
- Bring support hand up to high chest.
- Get a good grip on your firearm.
   1. Pull straight up and out of holster.
   2. Kant it a little sideways to keep the slide clear of clothing.
   3. Meet up with both hands. Get Off the X – Move to the side.
   4. Bring firearm up to your sight line.
Remember to always Scan and Assess the area and look at your holster before you re-holster your firearm.

Handgun Reloads:

- Emergency Reload - is when you get a slide lock and need to get ammo in your firearm right away.

- Tactical Reload - is because you want more ammo and have the cover or space/time to do the tactical reload.

Bring your elbow into your ribs, while keeping your eyes on the threat. Remember when you do a tactical reload that you still have a round in the chamber and can shoot if needed.

Malfunction Clearance:

A malfunction is an interruption in the cycle of operation of a semi-automatic pistol that can be cleared with an immediate action drill.

TYPE I - Fail to Fire: This type of malfunction most commonly occurs because the shooter failed to fully seat the magazine. This results in the slide not stripping a round off the top of the magazine and closing on an empty chamber.

This can also occur from defective ammunition, a broken firing pin, or the slide not going fully into battery (because the pistol is dirty and/or the shooter ran the slide gently when charging the chamber).

ANYTIME THE PISTOL PRODUCES THESE SYMPTOMS THE SHOOTER SHOULD IMMEDIATELY

TAP – strongly strike the bottom of the magazine with the open palm of the support hand to seat it fully.

RACK & CANT – rack/cant, to clear the chamber and to chamber a fresh round.

ASSESS – mental decision to fire/not fire the pistol, or otherwise finish the fight or drill.

Stove Pipe Malfunctions:

TYPE 2 – Failure to Eject - This malfunction commonly results from the shooter limp wrist the handgun, in other words, not locking the wrist on the strong side and permitting too much muzzle flip (rise) during recoil.

To Clear a Stove Pipe Malfunction: Wipe the Brass- Briskly wipe the brass from the ejection port, without running the slide and circle back with your support hand and establish a two-handed firing grip.

Over 90% of Type 2 malfunctions will have a fresh round chambering. If you run the slide in that situation, you can easily induce a Type 3 (double feed) malfunction. If your pistol does not have a fresh round chambering, and wiping the brass causes the slide to close on an empty chamber, a —**TAP-RACK-ASSESS** will get the pistol back into serviceable condition and the fight.

Stove Pipe Malfunction:

<u>Notes:</u>

____

____

____

____

____

____

____

____

____

Double Feed Malfunction:

LOOK- and FEEL to identify the malfunction. Tilt the muzzle upward to LOOK into the ejection port and FEEL with the trigger finger that the slide is back out of battery. (Normally, if the trigger finger is raised up onto the slide when it is in battery, you should feel the ejection port).

LOCK - the slide to the rear to ease pressure on the top round in the magazine if it is necessary for your pistol.

STRIP (or Rip) the magazine out of the magazine well.

RACK (rack, rack) - the slide vigorously 2 or 3 times to clear the chamber. Be careful not to cover the ejection port with your hand, this is the escape route for brass. Turn the pistol slightly to the right to assist clearance.

GLOCK Owners - Double Feed Fix - Tap rack pull magazine out reinsert a new magazine.

Example of Double Feed.

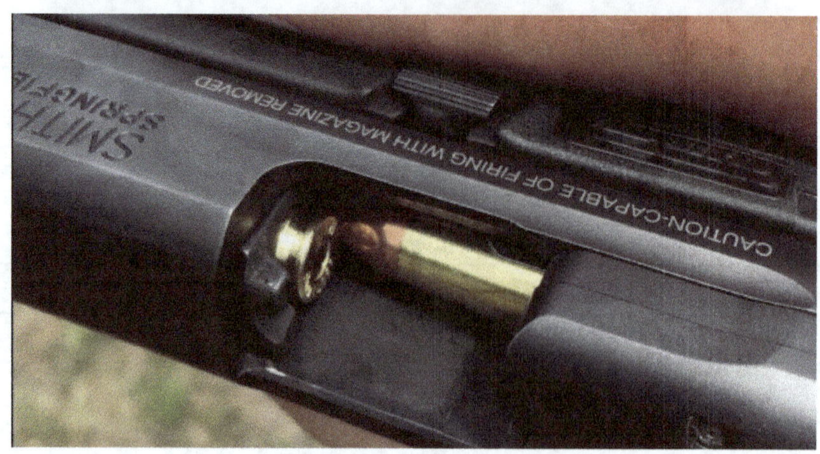

Flashlights:

According to FBI statistics, over 70% of shootings occur in low light. Are YOU prepared?

<u>**Why Train in Low light?**</u>
- 91% of engagements are within 21 feet, 67% within 10 feet.
- Average engagement is less than 2.5 seconds.
- 40% specifically ID lighting conditions as a contributing factor.
- 10% of training or less conducted at night (live fire).

<u>**The Human Eye Adaptation**</u>
- Dark adaptation- (Moving from light to dark)
- Slow - May be temporarily blind.
- 25 minutes – 80% adaptation.
- 60 minutes – 100% adaptation.

<u>**Light adaptation- (Moving from dark to light)**</u>
- Fast.
- 2 phases:
- Sensitivity of whole retina is decreased to ½ original sensitivity.
- Slower adaptation time leads to increased sensitivity (recovery).
- Example – walk out into bright sunlight.

<u>**Principles of Low- light Combat**</u>
- "Read" the light.
- Operate from the lowest level of light.
- Light and move.
- Power with light.
- Align three things.
- Carry more than one light.

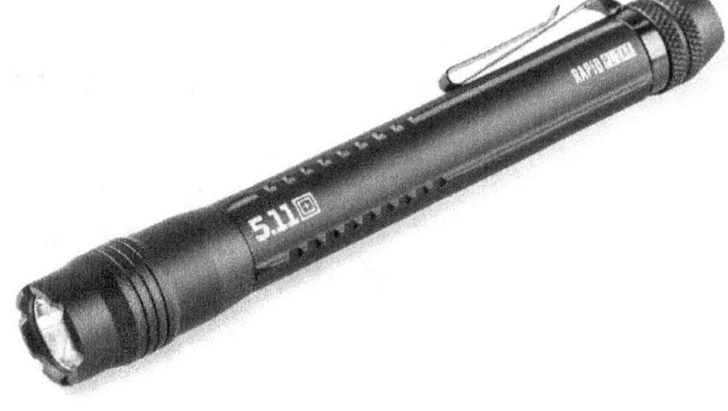

Handheld Flashlight:

FBI Technique

Harries Technique

Graham Technique

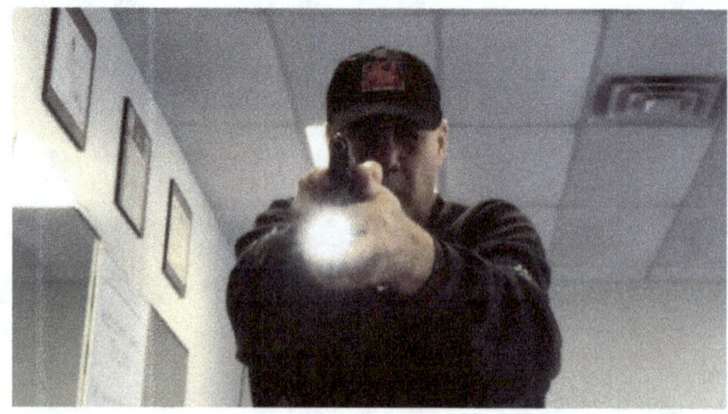

Weapon Mounted Light:

<u>Notes:</u>

____
____
____
____
____
____
____
____
____
____
____
____
____
____

Handgun as an Impact Tool:

Using your firearm as an impact tool is for situations where deadly force may not be the proper action or to create some space from your threat.

<u>Firearm Impact Points:</u>
- Muzzle
- Front Site
- Slide

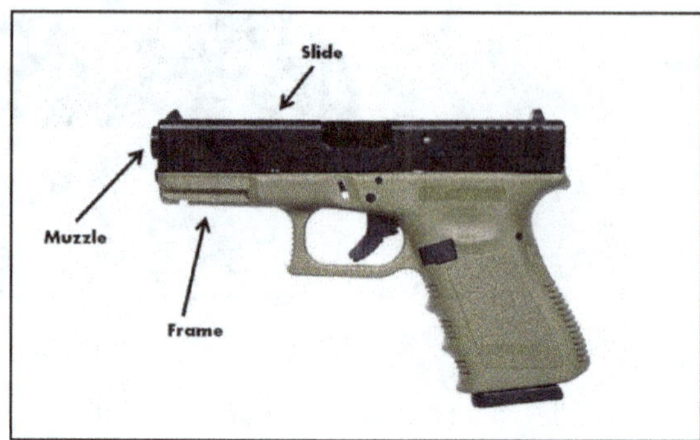

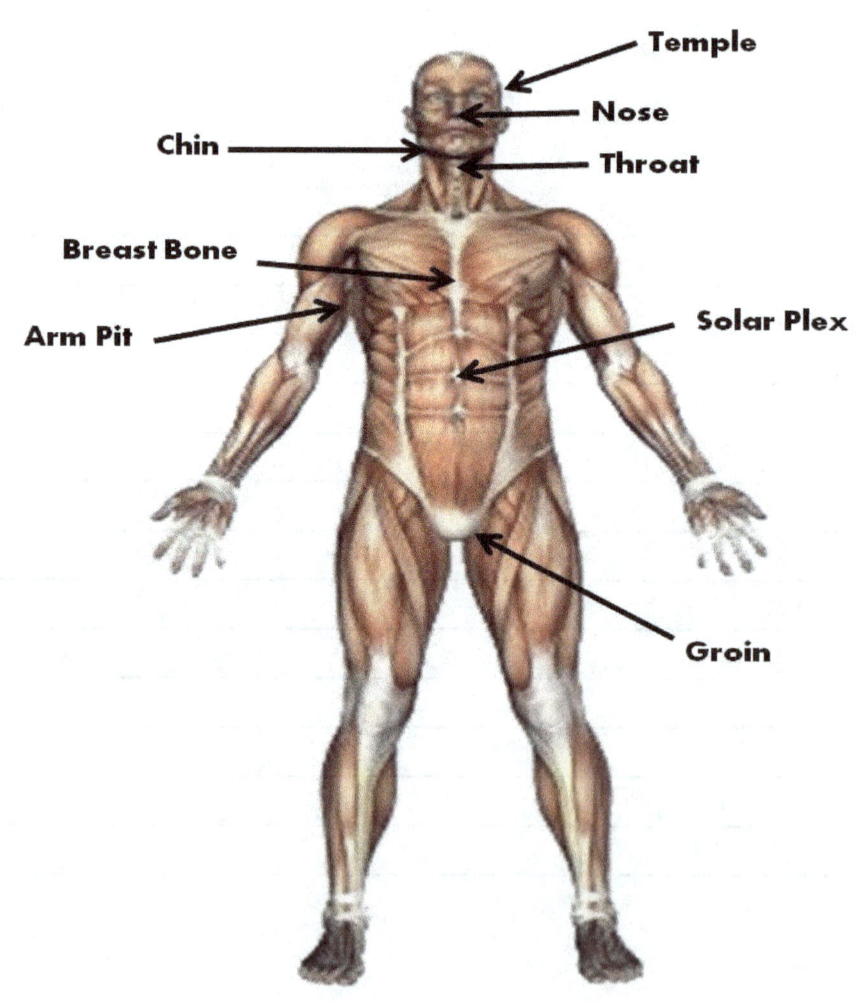

Vehicle Tactics:

Vehicle Fighting Priorities:

1 – **Escape in The Vehicle**
2 – **Use the Vehicle as a Weapon**
3 – **Bail Out of the Vehicle**
4 – **Fight from Within the Vehicle**

Shooting Out of your Windshield:

Your windshield is made up of two layers of glass sandwich between is a sheet of plastic.
- The plastic has a great effect on the bullet and how it will travel though.
- When shooting though glass there is **NO guarantee** on how the bullet will travel
- Your first shot whole purpose is to punch a hole through the glass.
- Ideally, we want the follow up shoots going through the same hole.

Shooting Out of your Windshield:

- Shooting through the windshield from outside your bullet will go down.
- Shooting through the windshield form the inside your bullet will travel up.
- The curvature of the windshield will also have a effect on the bullet.
- When you change the angle of shooting out of the windshield could also have an effect of making the bullet going left or right as well as going up.

Windshields:

The second major variable in shooting through a windshield is the angle of the glass. A bullet in flight is heavier in the rear than in the front. When the front of the bullet strikes glass at an angle (whether the trajectory of the bullet or the position of the glass creates the angle), the part of the bullet that touched the glass slows down first and causes the rear of the bullet to begin moving around to the front.

When the bullet breaks through the glass, it continues moving in that direction. In other words, shooting from the inside of a vehicle straight through the windshield, the first round typically strikes high on the target, if it hits the target at all.

Shooting Through Side & Rear Glass:

The side and rear windows of most modern vehicles are composed of tempered glass. When tempered glass breaks, it shatters into many small pieces. These small pieces are very sharp and will cause injury, but for the most part the injuries will be minor compared to if the glass broke into large shards.

When firing through tempered glass, the first shot will quite literally blow out the entire window. The glass will probably cause some degree of deflection of the first bullet, but that will vary depending on the bullet type, weight, angle of strike, etc. The ideal thing to do is fire multiple shots at the target … or a double tap at the very least.

<u>**Shooting Out of Your Side Windows:**</u>
The side windows are made of temper glass and will shatter into small pieces.
Shooting through the door glass could also have some impact on the directly of the bullet on the angle we are shooting it from.

Straight on will not have much of an impact on the direction of the bullet. Window tinting film will help keep the window from falling out. Bullet design will have a different outcome when they pass though.

<u>**FMJs -vs- Hollow Points Through Glass:**</u>
- Hollow points don't get as much penetration.
- FMJ will penetrate more.

<u>**Shooting Through Glass Covered by a Tinting Film:**</u>
If the tempered glass windows are covered by a tinting film, things change. The film acts to hold the small pieces of broken glass in place like interlocking puzzle pieces. The first shot fired will shatter the glass as before, but since the glass cannot fall out of place, the result is that the window becomes almost opaque, thereby obscuring your view of the target.

Expect to experience some degree of deflection every time a bullet strikes the film/glass unless bullets travel through pre-existing holes. The best option is to use something to knock the glass out once it has been broken. This can be time-consuming and dangerous.

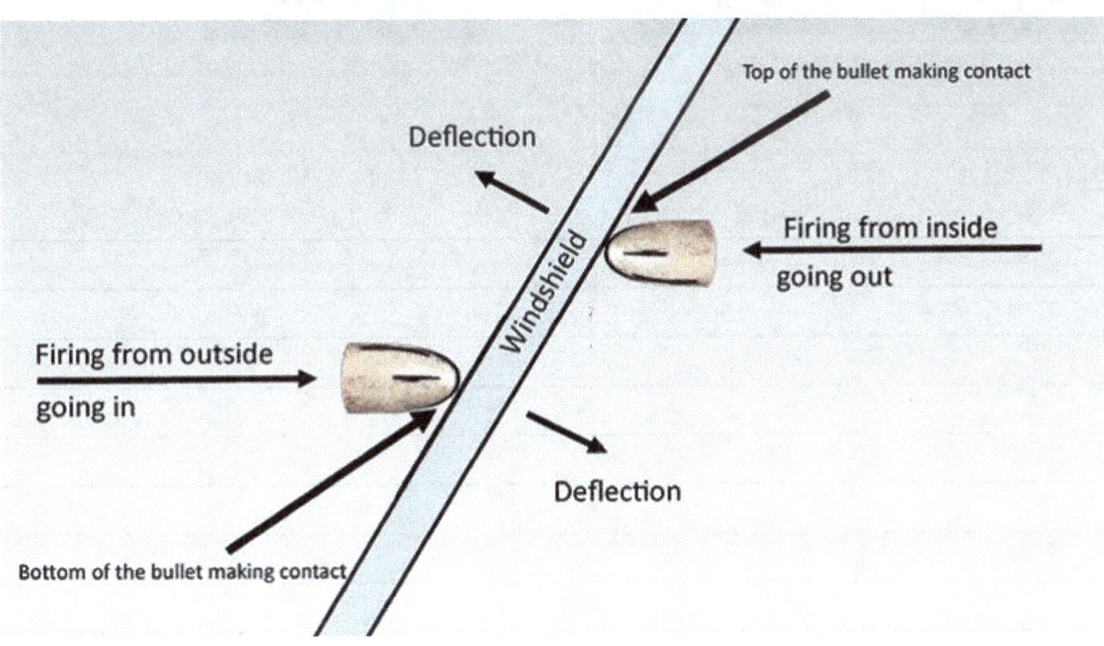

<u>**Response From Within the Vehicle:**</u>
If you are right-handed take your seat belt off with your left hand at the same time turn and lean towards your left side straightening out your right leg so you can access your Firearm.
Bring the Firearm up and over the top of the steering wheel so you are not muzzling yourself.

<u>**Shooting out the windshield:**</u>
- Lean back so you can push your arms out.

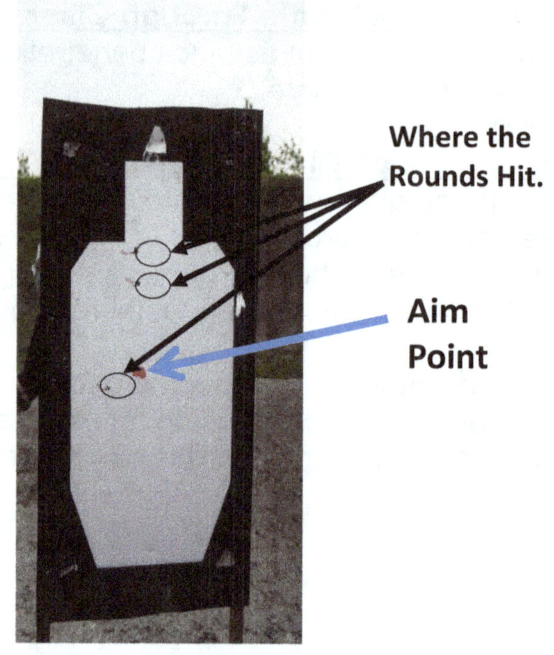

<u>Notes:</u>

____
____
____
____
____
____
____
____
____
____
____

Shooting out the driver's side window:

- Stay as low of a profile as possible-

Shooting out the passage side window:

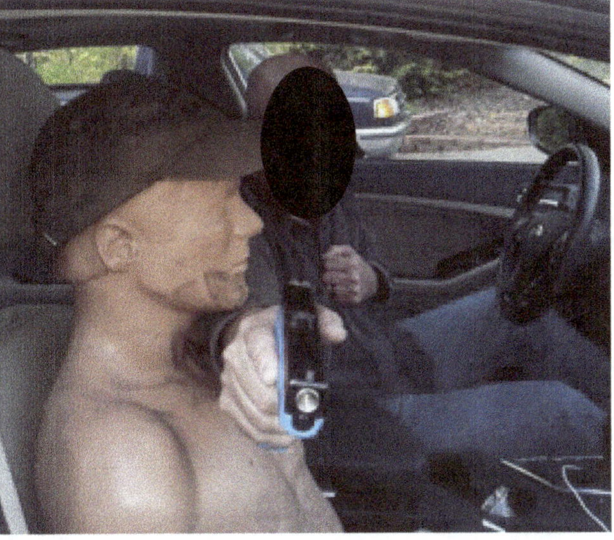

- Lean to the left and turn towards the window.

Shooting around the vehicle:

- Stay as low of a profile as possible-

<u>Notes:</u>

Room Clearing

Super "T" Tactical Room

This room is designed so the inside walls can be moved and changed around to set up different layouts when doing room clearing techniques.

Room Clearing

You must be under control when clearing a room. Split second decisions must be made to identify threats when encountered.

Look Up, Down, in closets, behind furniture, desk, etc.

What type of a threat is present?
- Are they attacking you?
- Do they have a weapon?
- Are they friend, family member?

All these aspects must be considered before determining your action.

Threat Area
When clearing a building, EVERYTHING NOT in the vicinity of you as you proceed is the "Threat Area".

Danger Area
The Danger Area created by opening such as entry onto property in view of a building, primary door entry ways, all interior doors, stairwells, crawl spaces, attic hatches, windows, etc. Any area that can restrict movement and provides no cover is a danger area. **DO NOT** linger or hedge when you reach the point that you are exposed, move quickly but only move as fast as you can effectively shoot.

Room Entry / Clearing
When entering a room **COMMIT** to it, do so with all the advantages on your side, keep a good mental state of mind, expect to find someone every time.

Slicing the Pie:

<u>**Slicing the Corner:**</u>
- Be Patient
- Inch Slowly
- Move Muzzle up and down searching for your threat
- Search and scan every possible hiding spot

<u>**Limited Penetration**</u>
Using the protection of the corner of the hallway. Slowly approach the corner, focusing on the corner with weapon pointed at the threat area. Stop momentarily, then make a deliberate move around the corner maximizing the protection of the corner.

You may also utilize a "quick peak" around the corner before moving around the corner. (If you do more than one "quick peak", be sure to do them at different heights.

Angle of Incidence (slicing the pie)

Allows you to observe a major portion of the hallway from around the corner. Approach the corner using entire width of the hallway.

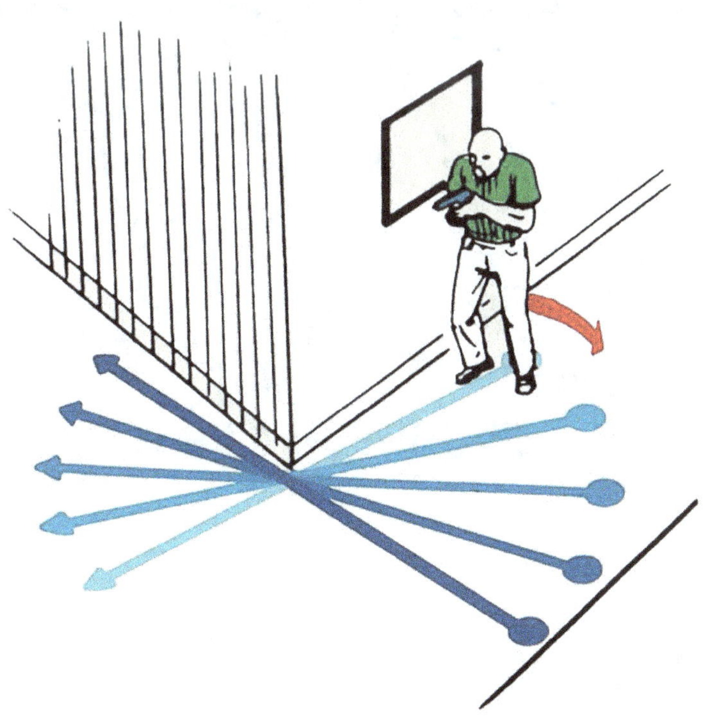

Fatal Funnel:

Doorways:
- Be Patient
- Inch Slowly
- Move Muzzle up and down searching for your threat
- Search and scan every possible hiding spot

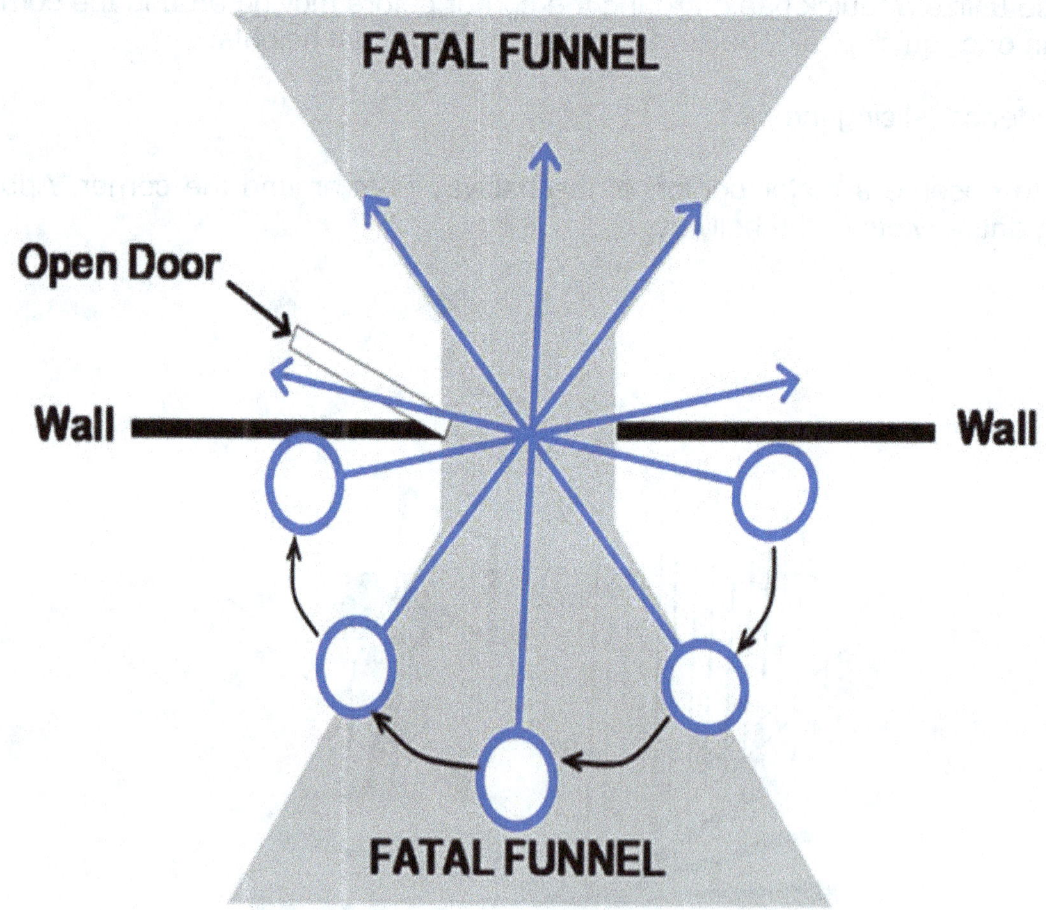

Stairways:

Stairways are to be cleared slow and deliberately. AVOID THESE IF POSIBLE
 As you climb the stairs use angles to cut the pie to observe as much ahead of them as they can.
- Inch Slowly
- Move Muzzle up and down searching for your threat
- Search and scan every possible hiding spot

<u>Clearing Tactics:</u>

Slow and Deliberate: The goal of slow and deliberate is to reach the location without being detected. (Not all parts of this technique are slow, you must move fast at certain times such as through a danger area. Stealth is the greatest consideration)

Dynamic: Performed at a greater rate of speed, to quickly overwhelm the adversaries. (Often used in response to a hostage being seriously harmed or to keep adversaries from setting up and barricading further also used in Active Shooter situations.)

Key elements of Dynamic Building Clearing:
- Speed: A faster moving target is harder to hit than a slower one.
- Surprise: Make the subject react to you.
- Shock Action: Keep subject(s) mentally off balance, overwhelm their senses so they begin to think about reactions. It is achieved through explosive breaching, aggressiveness of the team.
- If you are going to commit, then do so with all the advantages on your side.
- Sound and voice discipline, don't telegraph your presence and/or movements.
- Use a distraction if available.
- Keeping a good mental state of mind – if/when you go into an area expect to find someone every time. Do not doubt it and be caught un-prepared as a result.

<u>Notes:</u>

____

____

____

____

____

____

____

____

____

Remember to Teach Your Kids:

Super T EDC
Tactical Knife
Predator Defense

Predator Defensive Knife System:

Real World: Most Knife systems teach Knife on Knife self-defense, but most stabbings are an ambush where the person never sees the knife.

All Knife systems have some good to offer and can be of value. The Super T Defense Predator Defense System will integrate with all Knife systems to help and give the practitioner more real-world knowledge.

The predator defense system utilizes biomechanical cutting to eliminate the use of the muscle / tendons so one may make an escape without having to inflict deadly force when not being necessary.

By cutting particular muscle groups you will eliminate certain functions of the muscle
" example " when you cut the wrist flexors you will not be able to close the hand thus making impossible for the attacker to hold on to you.

Fantasy Vs Reality Knife Attacks
Knife attacks are just like empty hand in the nature that they are repetitive and brutal never a single stab/slash, as never a single strike. You must train as if everyone has a knife in their hands trying to stab, slice and kill you!

This book is for reference ONLY. To really understand using the knife for Self Defense you need to train under a qualified Instructor.

Super T Knife Grips

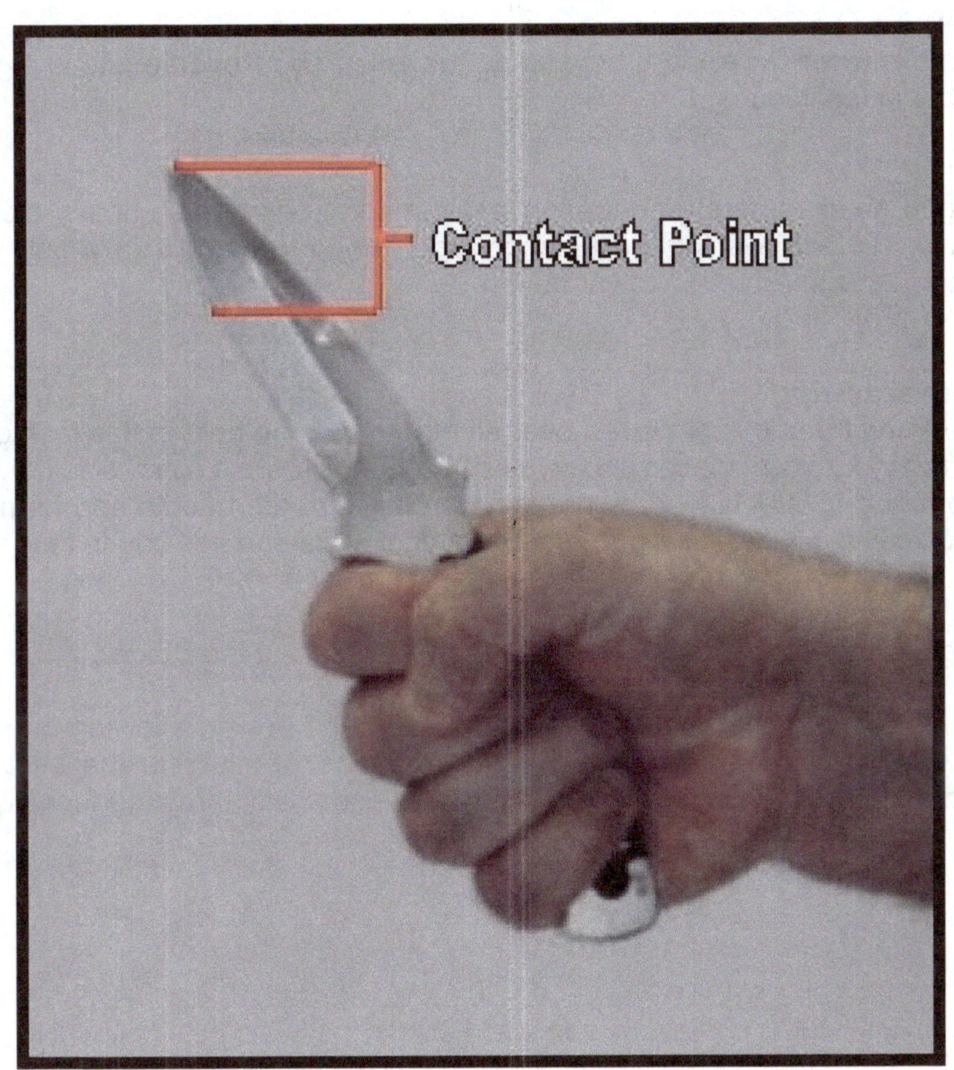

Super T Knife Grips

Knife Grips:
The terrain and environment are rarely ideal for close combat. Rain, mud or snow will make the handle of a knife slippery and difficult to manage, and wearing gloves only makes it more difficult to wield the weapon efficiently.

Reverse Grip:
The reverse grip is when the knife is held along the wrist. The Reverse grip is a great grip for in close and stabbing techniques.

Ice-Pick grip:
The Ice-pick grip enables deep penetration against soft body armor, heavy clothing, or other protective outfits. To achieve this grip, simply hold the knife handle in a fist, with the blade pointing down and the sharp edge towards you.

Hammer / Forward Grip:
The Hammer / Forward grip is preferred over all others. A knife held in this fashion is less likely to be knocked from your grasp and can also be used in conjunction with a punch or to deliver butt-end knife strikes. A Hammer grip is achieved by grasping the knife at the handle and forming a tight fist. Keep the wrist flexible, as if using a hammer or hatchet. This enables you to lock the wrist tightly when needed.

The Forward grip up lace your thumb in line with the top part of the Blade.

The Hammer / Forward grip provides great penetration and power, allowing the blade to easily cut through heavy clothing. There is also less likelihood of injury to the user's thumb. The hammer grip can be used for chopping, slashing, and especially thrusting techniques.

Reverse Grip

Reverse Grip:
Thumb on top of the
handle blade pointed
towards the target.
- Range Close Quarters

Ice Pick Grip:
Thumb on top of the
handle blade pointed
towards you.
- Range Close Quarters

Forward Grip

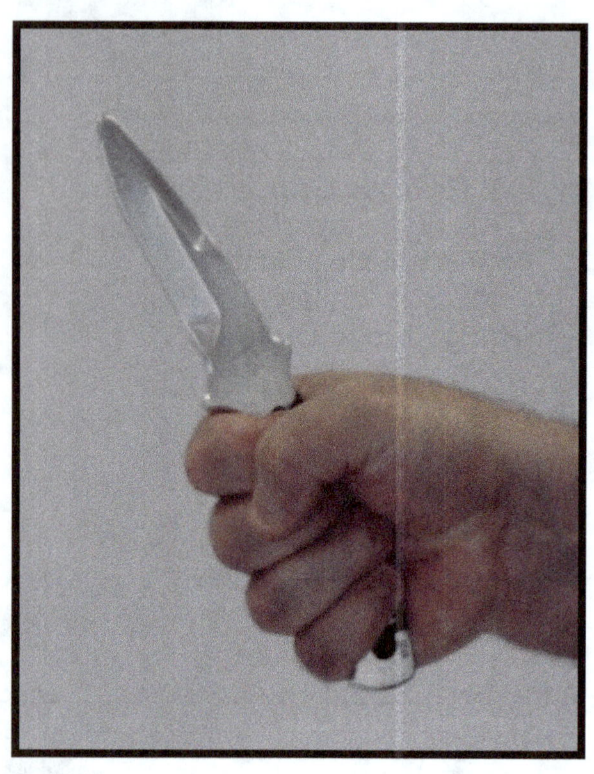

Hammer Grip:
Grip the handle like you
would a hammer.
- Range Outside -

Forward Grip:
Grip the handle with the
thumb on top of
the blade.
- Range Outside -

Impact Grip

Knife in the Closed Position
Notice how it sticks out of the top and bottom of
the hand so it can be used as an Impact tool.
- Range Close Quarters -

<u>Notes:</u>

Super T Knife Stances

Stances:

Stance:
After achieving an effective grip, the knife fighter must assume an appropriate combat stance. The stance is much like a modified boxer's stance to help give you more mobility.

Covering:
Covering means hiding behind your knife by keeping the weapon between you and your opponent. By keeping the knife pointed toward the enemy, you can attack and/or block or parry any thrusts by the opponent. You can also pull the weapon close to your body, leaving your free hand to protect against an opponent's grabbing technique.

Shield Hand
The knife fighter's free hand should be held close to the heart or solar plexus to protect vital areas such as the heart and throat. Should the enemy's blade get through your defenses, your freehand will hopefully absorb the blade rather than one of your vital organs. This technique is taken from Filipino Escrima, in which the hand is used as a shield and is sacrificed, if necessary. Maybe used to parry, punch, fake a blow, throw objects, distract the opponent, or assist balance in rough terrain

Notes:

Stances:

Knife in Forward grip in the back hand. Cover your Vitals with your free hand.

Knife in Forward grip in the front hand. Cover your Vitals with your free hand.

Stances:

Knife in Reverse grip in the back hand. Cover your Vitals with your free hand.

Knife in Reverse grip in the front hand. Cover your Vitals with your free hand.

Forward Grip Knife Set #1

Forward Grip Set #1:

<u>Super T Forward Set #1</u>
1 - Angle slash down
2 - Angle slash down
3 - Across slash
4 - Across slash
5 - Straight stab
6 - Reverse eye Polk
7 - Eye poke
8 - Up stab
9 - Reinforced cut
10 - Groin stab

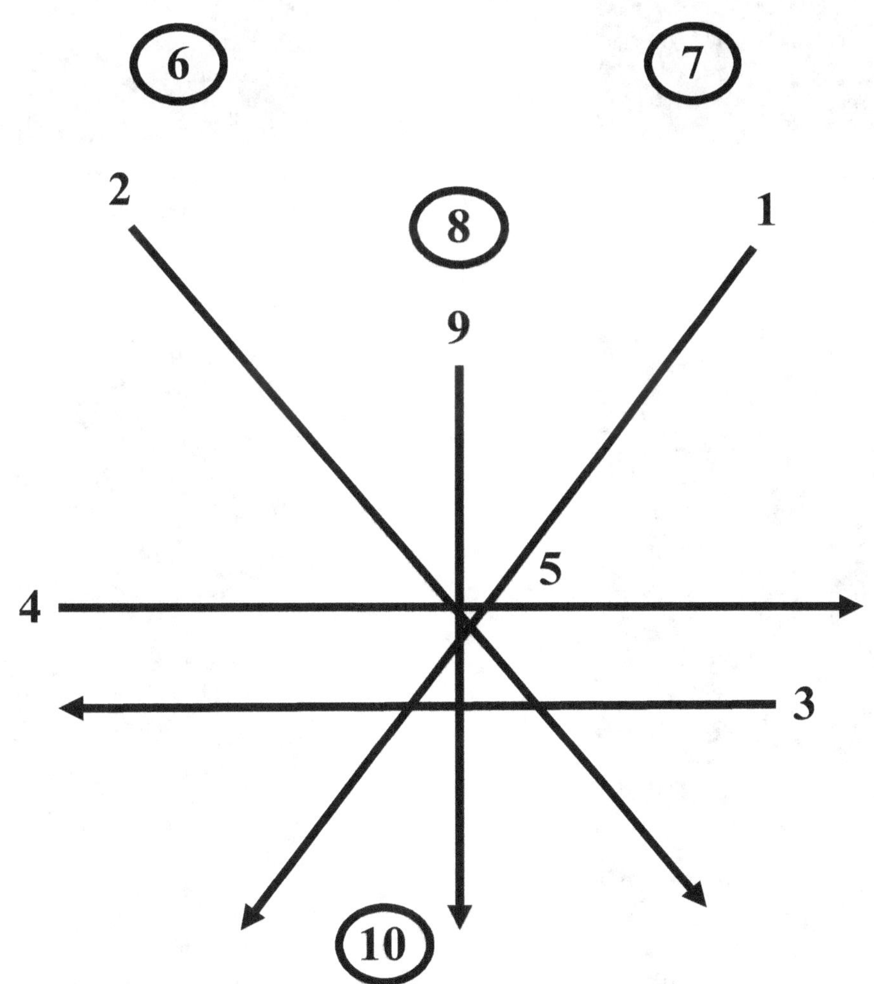

Forward Set:

#1 Angle slash from the Left shoulder down.

#2 Angle slash from the Right shoulder down.

#3 Across slash going from the Right to the Left.

#4 Across slash going from the Left to the Right.

Forward Set:

#5 Straight stab to the Solar Plexus.

#6 Stab to the Right eye.

#7 Stab to the Left eye.

#8 Stab to the chin.

Forward Set:

#9 Reinforce slash down the body.

#10 Groin Stab.

Notes:
____
____
____
____
____
____
____
____
____
____
____

Reverse Grip Knife Set #1

Reverse Grip Set #1:

Super T Reverse Set #1

1 - Straight stab stomach
2 - Across slash
3 - Across slash
4 - Body stab
5 - Body Stab
6 - Upward slash
7 - Down stab
8 - Downward slash
9 - Groin stab

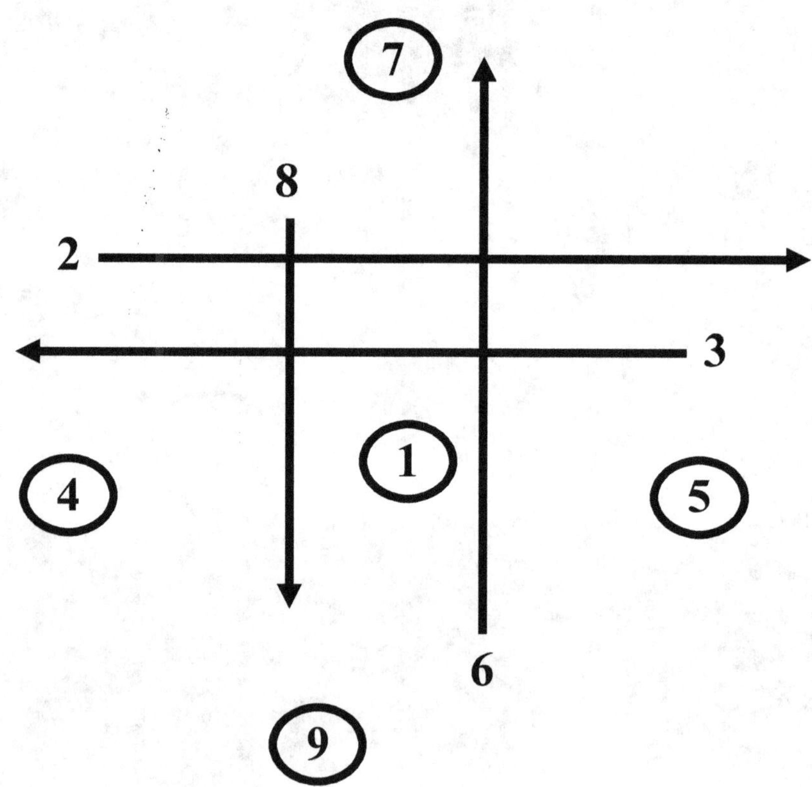

Reverse Set:

#1 Straight stab to the Solar Plexus.

#2 Slash across the throat.

#3 Slash across the throat.

#4 Stab to the Right side of the chest.

Reverse Set:

#5 Stab to the Left side of the chest.

#6 Straight up the face slash.

#7 Stab to the top of the head.

#8 Reverse down slash.

Reverse Grip Knife Sets

#9 Groin Stab.

Notes:

Upper Body Distraction Cutting:

Distraction cutting is a way of disrupting the mechanical function of the body. It does not mean to end or terminate life. It is simply a way to shut the function of the attacker down

If you can stop the mechanical function of your attacker, then things become clear in combative reality.

• If the threat of their attack is removed, hopefully it will stop the attackers desire to continue their assault.

• If the attacker's mobility is destroyed, one's escape can be implemented, as they cannot follow.

• The attacker's condition can be deterrent to others wanting to take similar action.

• Legal ramifications may possibly be kept to a minimum.

WARNING:

Correct Mentality
When someone carries a knife for self-defense that person must be prepared to use that knife with lethal effect if necessary. In a self-defense scenario there should be no doubt that the attacker intends to perform serious bodily damage, to prevent that from happening the knife user should be prepared to take any action necessary for self-defense with avoidance being top priority.

Targets
There are three major target groups in a knife fight, muscles and nerves, blood vessels and vital organs. Severing the muscles and nerves disables the attacker's limbs eventually achieving the purpose of self-defense. Severing blood vessels and vital organs causes eventual death.

Wrist & Finger Flexors

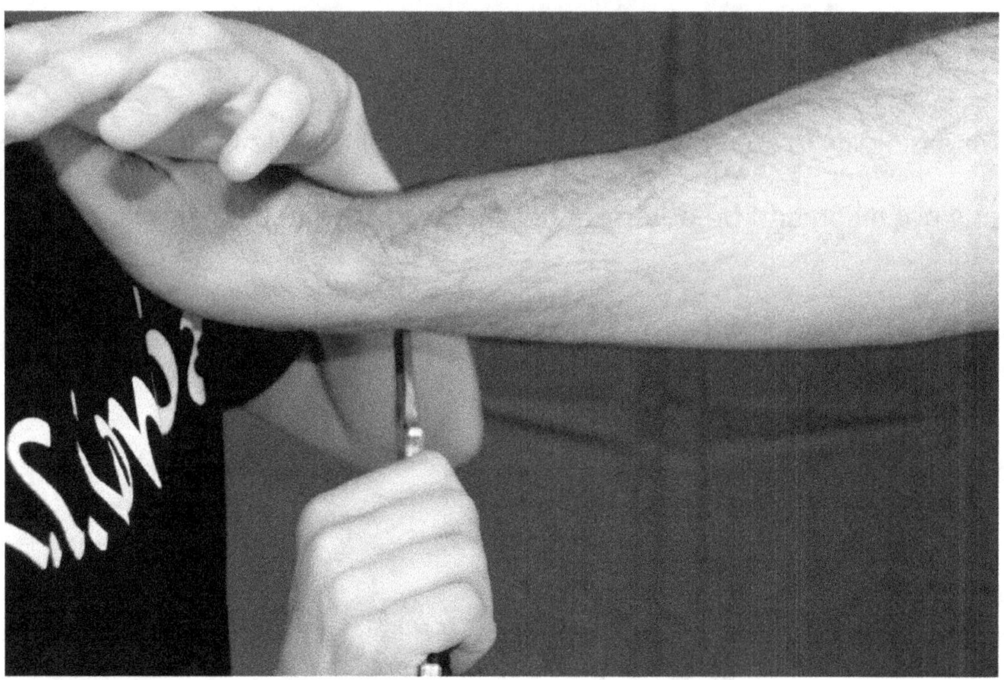

Arm Biceps:

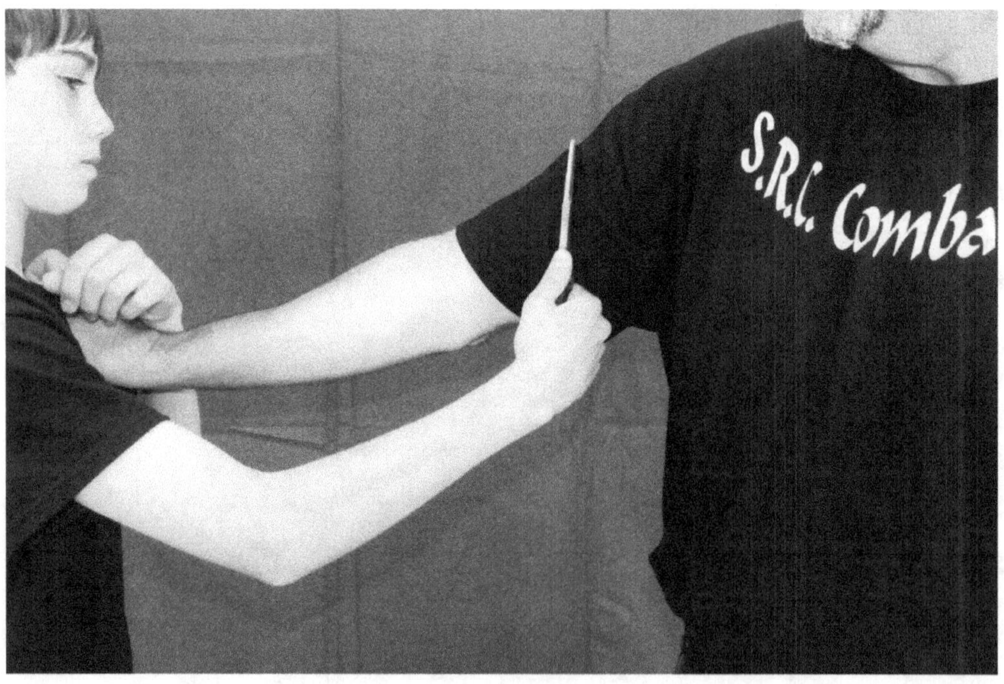

Latissimus Dorsi Muscle:

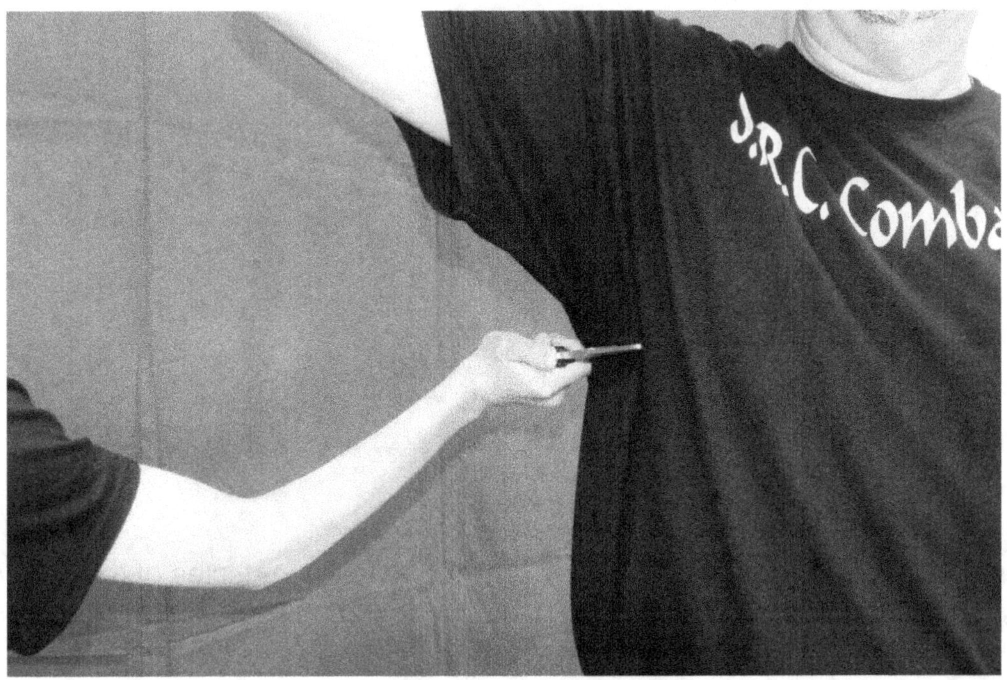

Trapezius:

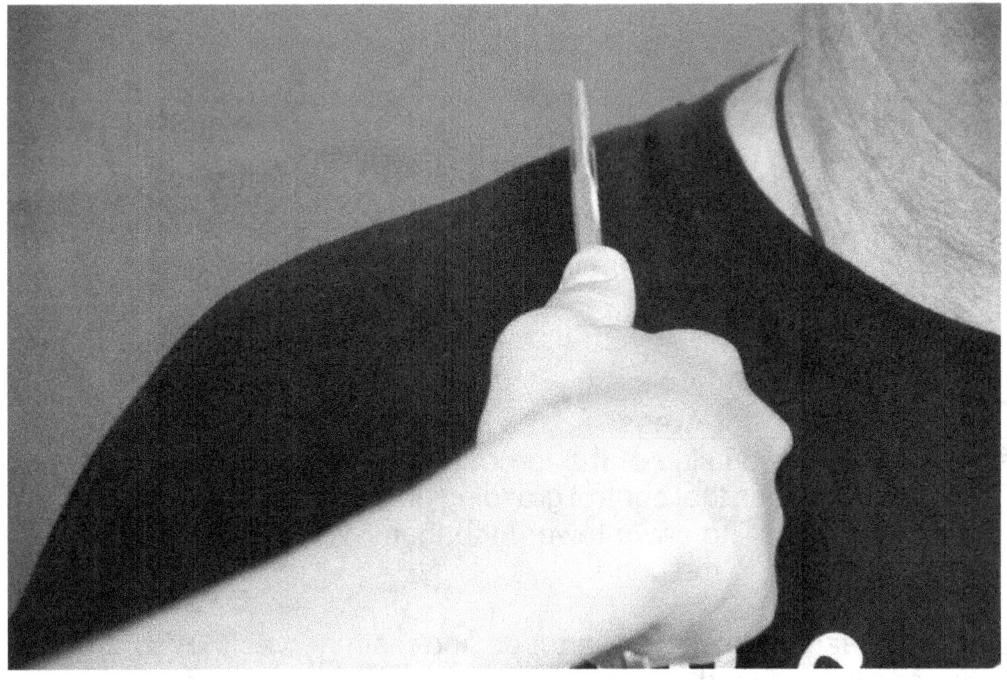

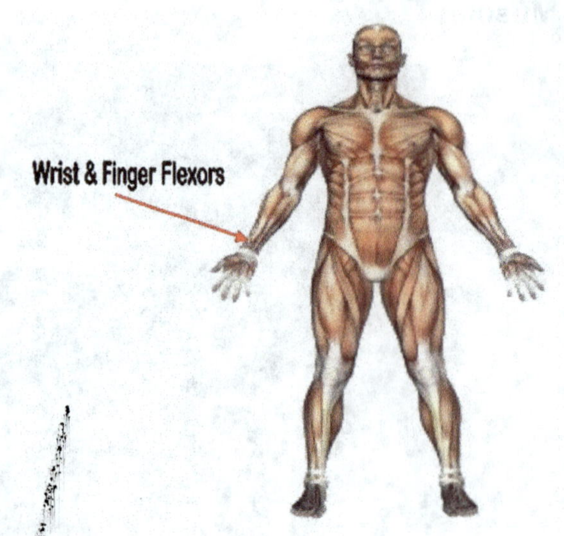

Wrist & Finger Flexors:

The attacker's ability to gasp or grab a hold of you is due to the muscles of the hand/wrist/fingers working together. A complex dynamic between nerves, muscle, and tendons is needed to sustain the grip. By cutting the wrist flexors, the attacker will lose the ability to hold onto you.

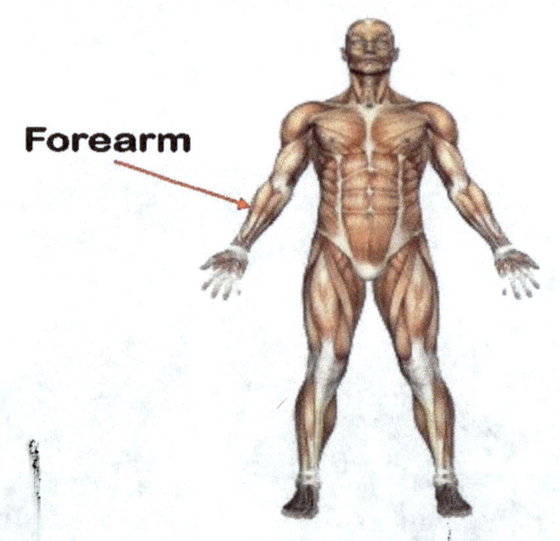

The Forearm Has Many Target Areas:

• Cutting the muscles on the outside of the forearm cuts the extensors, which uncurl or extend the fingers. The nerve functions that control grasping are located on the outside as well. Catching a cut up by the elbow and pulling down toward the thumb can send a fillet over the opponent's hand. The fillet may go down to the bone.

• Cutting the inside forearm contains the arteries and main nerves that control the wrist and the fist. Severing the nerves and /or the muscles will cause the flexors, which keep the hand closed not to work, or will destroy the needed nerve impulses to accomplish the same function. Fillets can be cut from the inside of the forearm as well as the outside forearm.

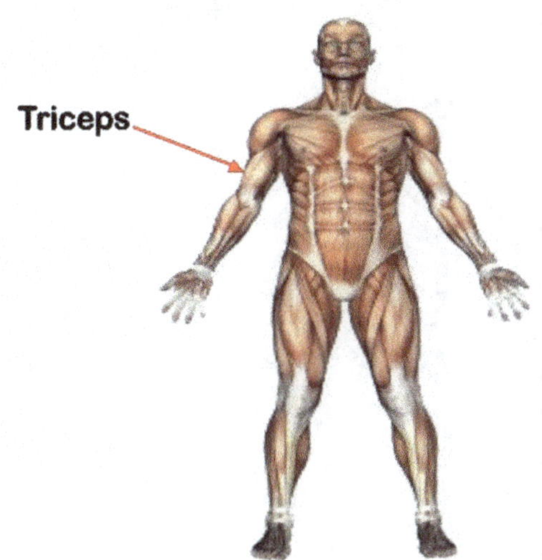

Triceps:
The triceps brachii muscle (Latin for "three-headed arm muscle") is the large muscle on the back of the upper limb of many vertebrates. It is the muscle principally responsible for extension of the elbow joint (straightening of the arm).

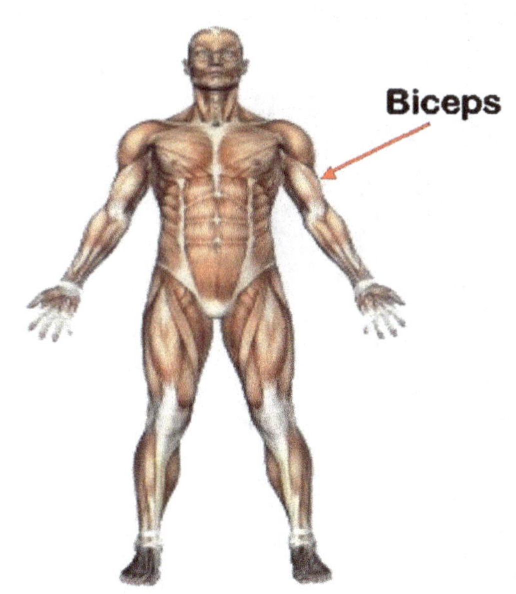

Arm Biceps:
The biceps lie on the upper arm between the shoulder and the elbow. The biceps' main function is to flex the elbow and rotate the forearm. By cutting the Biceps it can stop the attacker from pulling you in.

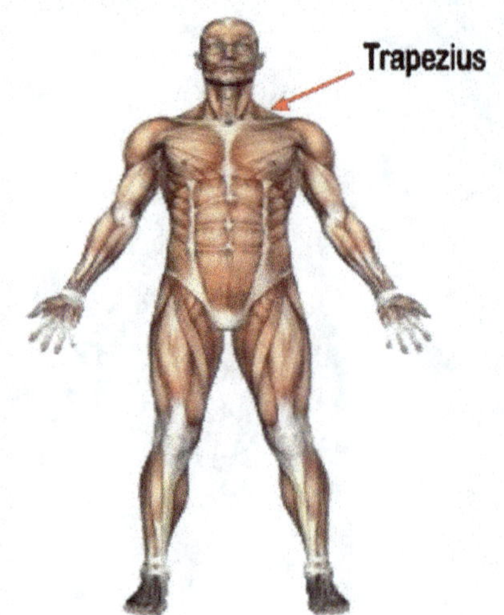

Trapezius:

The trapezius supports the weight of the arm as well as retracting the scapula and the inferior region rotating and depressing the stability of the arm.

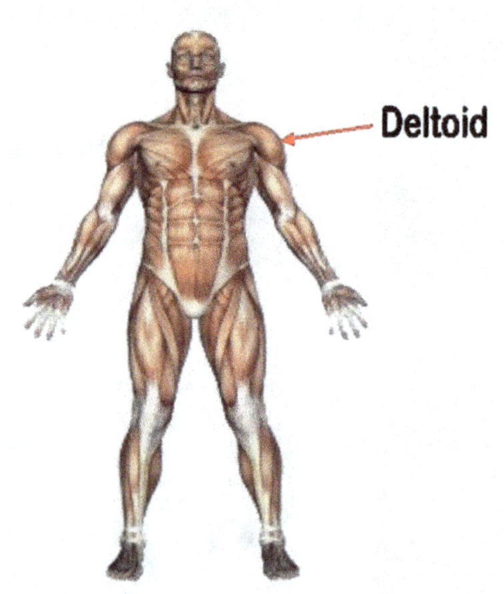

Deltoid:

The deltoid is responsible for lifting the arm.

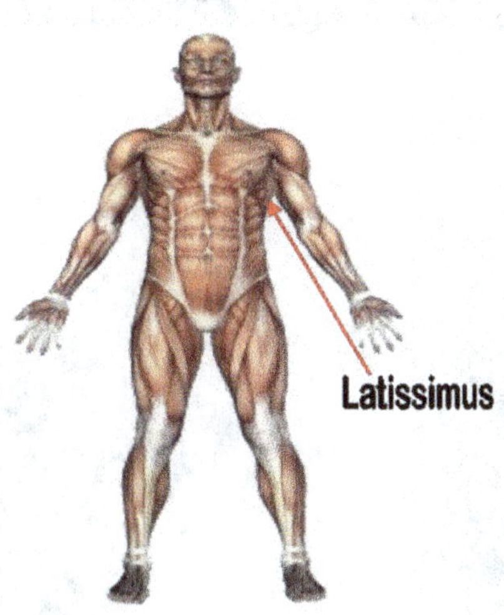

Latissimus Dorsi Muscle:
The latissimus dorsi is responsible for the downward rotation during a rollup.

Notes:

____
____
____
____
____
____
____
____
____
____
____
____
____
____
____
____

Lower Body Distraction Cutting:

Sartorius / Hip Flexors:

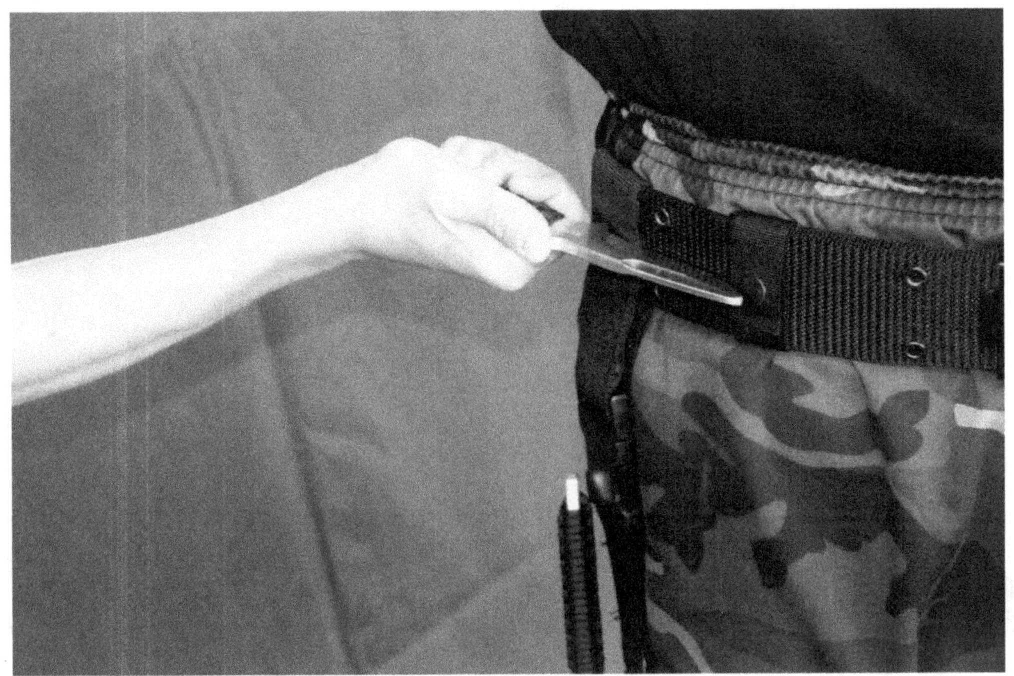

Quadriceps:

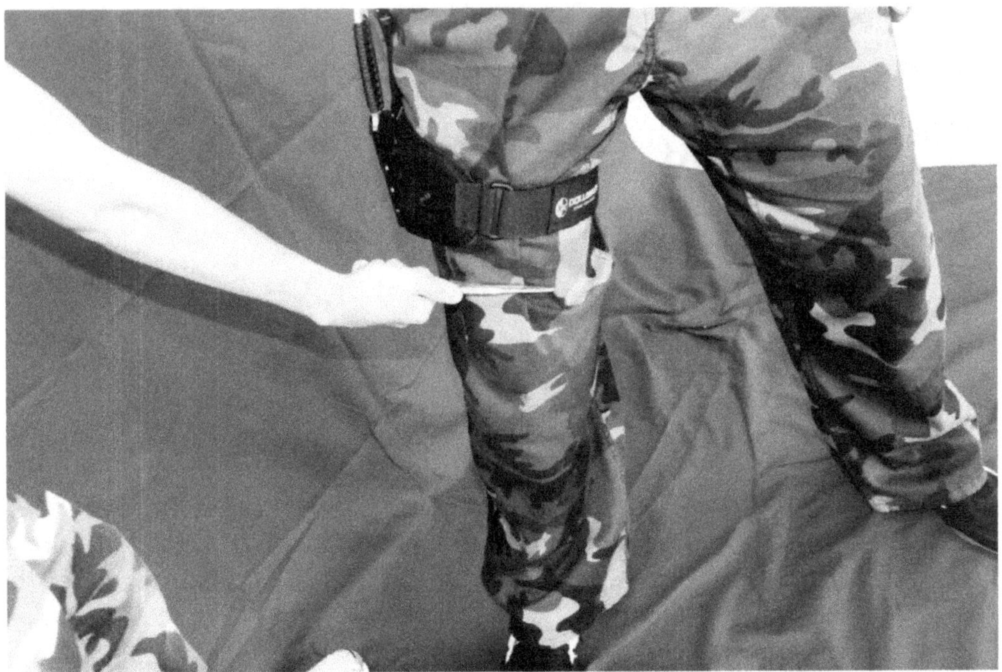

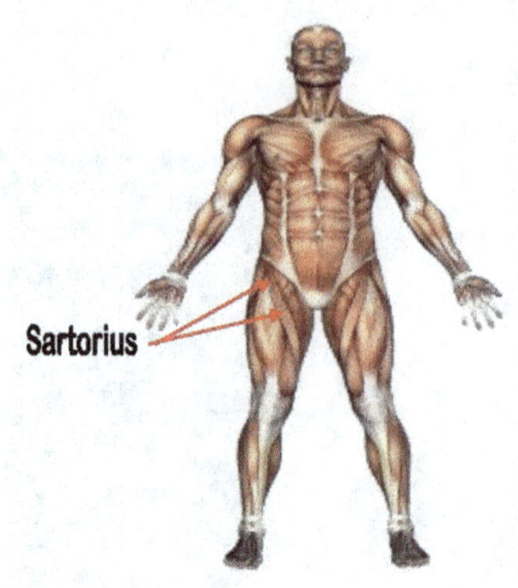

Sartorius:

The Sartorius muscle – the longest muscle in the human body – is a long thin muscle that runs down the length of the thigh. Assists in flexing, abduction and lateral rotation of hip, and flexion of knee. Cutting this muscle will make it difficult for the attacker to bend their leg and move it away from the body. This will make it so they may not be able to take chase after you.

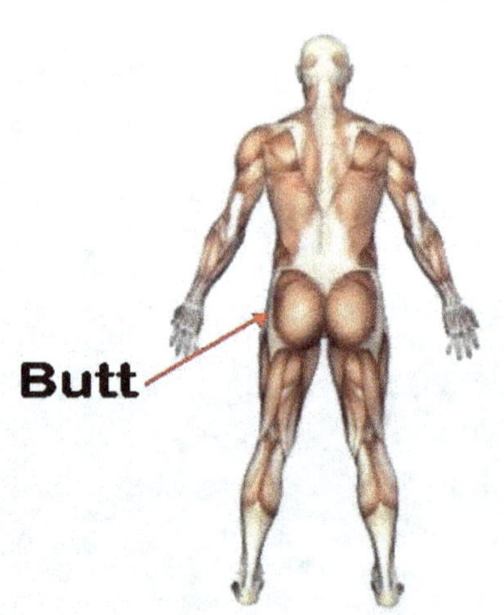

The Butt - Glutes:

One of the largest muscle groups in the body is the Gluts. When the Gluts are incapacitated, the body cannot move. One needs the Gluts to be able to stand, move, walk, run, and pivot. Poking the opponents butt with the tip of one's knife can cause immediate stoppage of the opponent's movement

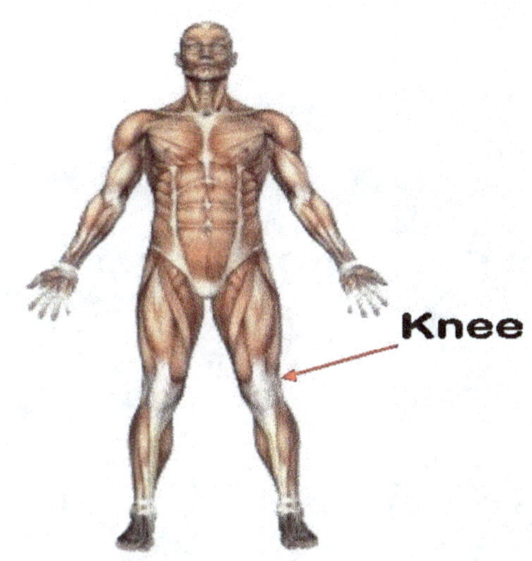

The Knee - Fragile Hinged Joint:

Cutting the "knee" causes severe damage and bio-mechanically if the knee doesn't work, the body stays in one place. The knee cannot bend nor can the hip flex. The thick cords felt behind the knee are the end of the hamstrings and they control extension of the hip. Cutting through these muscles takes little effort.

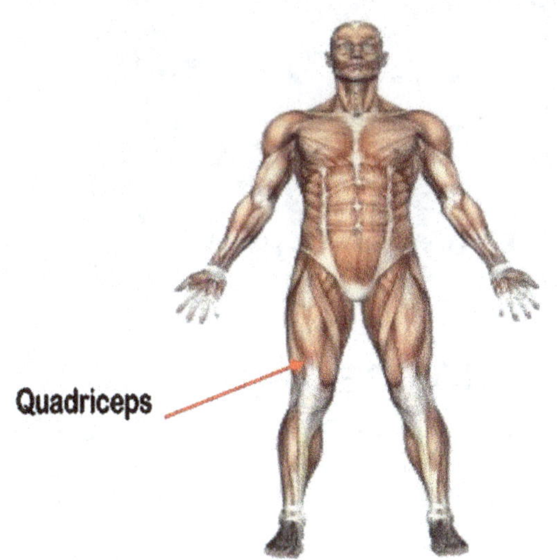

Quadriceps:

The quad muscles act to extend the knee joint, necessary to walk / run.

Arteries

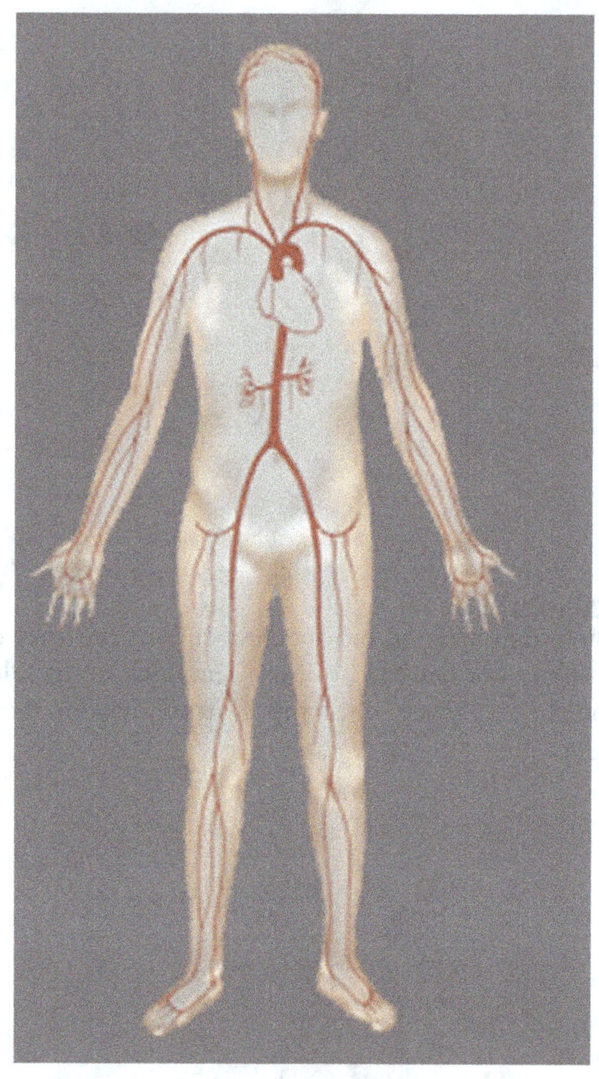

NOTICE:
-- By cutting these arteries the results could be immediate and deadly --

Carotid Artery:
Unconsciousness 5 seconds,
death 12 seconds.

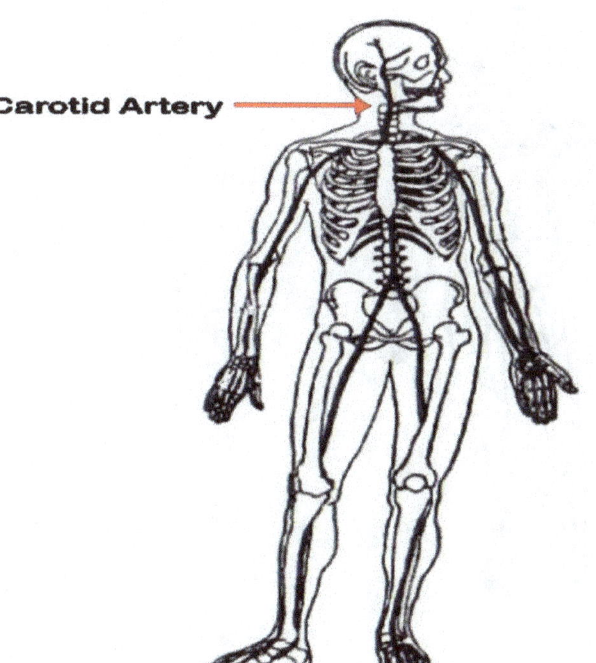

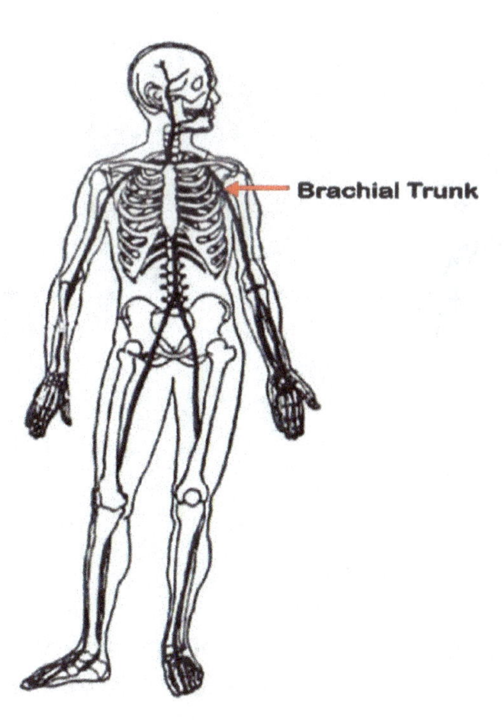

Brachial Artery:
Unconsciousness 14 seconds,
death 1.5 minutes.

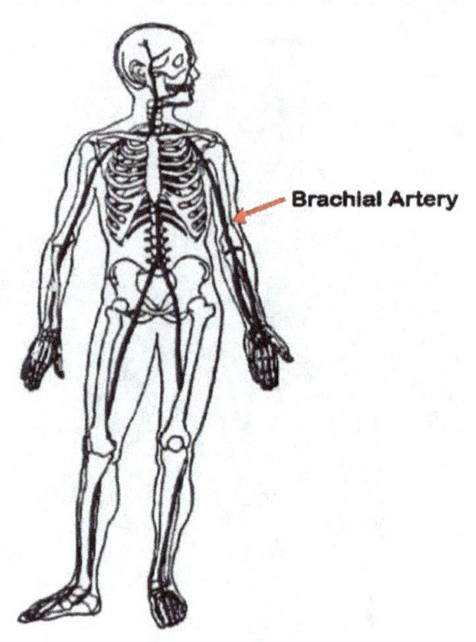

Brachial Artery:
Unconsciousness 14 seconds, death 1.5 minutes.

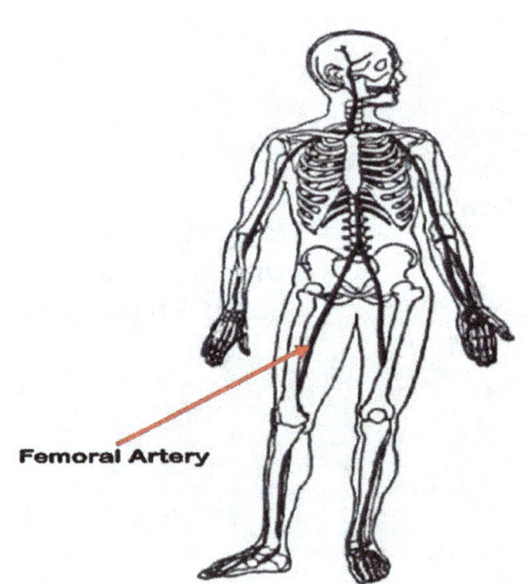

Femoral Artery:
The femoral artery is a main artery in the body that runs from the external iliac artery, near the stomach, all the way down both legs. It carries oxygen and nutrients to the lower half of the body. Vital to survival, if cut, an average person will typically bleed to death within 10 or 15 minutes without immediate medical intervention. Whenever this artery is injured, it becomes a life and death situation. The same holds true for all arteries because they carry much of the body's blood supply

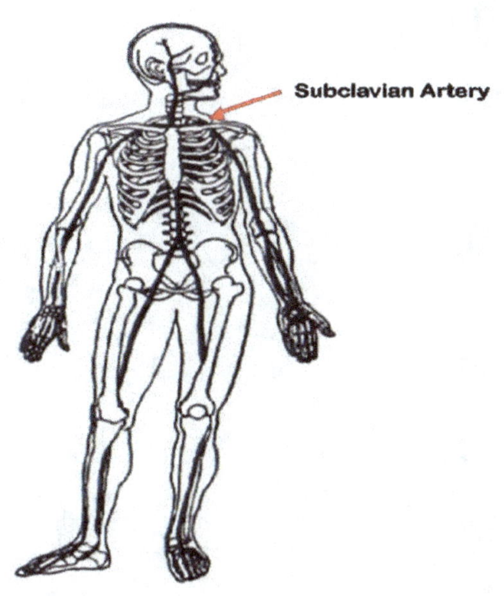

<u>Subclavian Artery:</u>
Unconsciousness 2 seconds, death 3.5 seconds.

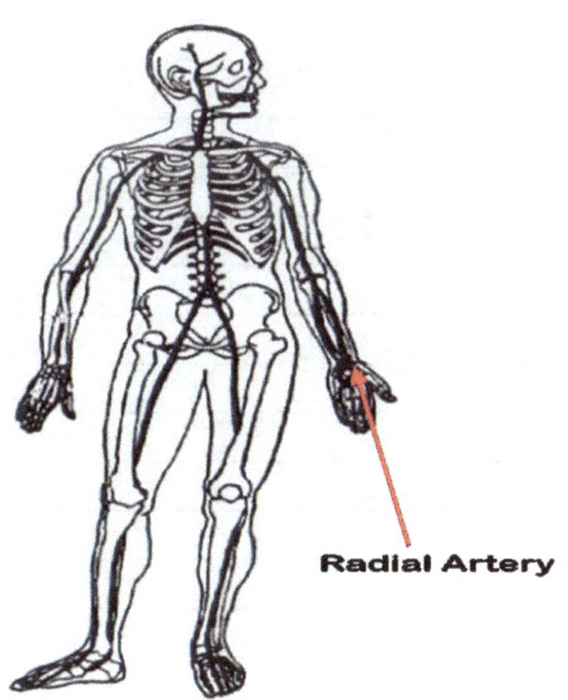

<u>Radial Artery:</u>
Unconsciousness 30 seconds, death 2 minutes.

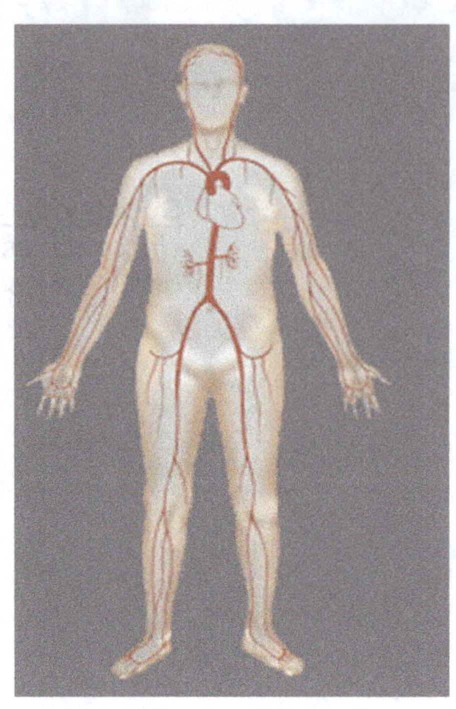

<u>Notes:</u>

PD Set #1 Forward Grip

BE SAFE

GET REAL

#1 As soon as you are grabbed take your Left hand and pin the grabbing hand to your chest.

#2 Immediately cut the wrist flexors.

#3 Use your Left arm and push there arm away from you keeping your hand up.

#4 Cut the Hip flexors so they can't chase you on your escape.

PD Set #1 Reverse Grip

#1 As soon as you are grabbed take your Left hand and pin the grabbing hand to your chest.

#2 Immediately cut the wrist flexors.

#3 Use your Left arm and push there arm away from you keeping your hand up.

#4 Cut the Hip flexors so they can't chase you on your escape.

PD Set #2 Forward Grip

#1 As soon as you are grabbed take your Left hand and pin the grabbing hand to your chest.

#2 Immediately cut the wrist flexors.

#3 Cut the Biceps.

#4 Push the arm away from your body.

#5 Cut the Hip Flexors so you can make your escape.

<u>Notes:</u>

PD Set #2 Reverse Grip

#1 As soon as you are grabbed take your Left hand and pin the grabbing hand to your chest.

#2 Immediately cut the wrist flexors.

#3 Use your Left arm and push their arm away from you keeping your hand up.

#4 Stab the Biceps.

#5 Cut the Quadriceps above the knee.

Notes:

PD Set #3 Forward Grip

#1 As soon as you are grabbed take your Left hand and pin the grabbing hand to your chest.

#2 Immediately filet up the arm.

#3 Cut the trap.

#4 Cut the lat.

PD Set #3 Reverse Grip

#1 As soon as you are grabbed take your Left hand and pin the grabbing hand to your chest.

#2 Immediately filet up the arm.

#3 Stab to the trap.

#4 Cut the lat.

#1 As soon as you are grabbed by two hands - Cut the Left Wrist Flexes.

#2 Drive the left arm down with your elbow.

#3 Cut the Right Biceps.

#4 Cut the Right Wrist Flexors.

#5 Push the arm away from your body.

#6 Cut the right Hip Flexors.

<u>Notes:</u>

PD Set #4 Reverse Grip

#1 As soon as you are grabbed by two hands - Cut the Left Wrist Flexes.

#2 Drive the left arm down with your elbow and stab the Right Biceps.

#3 Cut the Right Wrist Flexors.

#5 Push the arm away from your body.

#6 Cut the Right Hip Flexors.

Notes:

____
____
____
____
____
____
____
____
____
____
____
____
____
____

Self Defense
For the Real World

The following are several variation/options in a Self-Defense situation. They all come from the grips and predator sets. Never Limit yourself or options.

- Options -

Parry the Punch and counter with
a Stab to the Neck.

Parry the Punch and counter with
a Stab to the Lung.

Perry the Punch and counter with
a Stab to the Brachial Artery.

Duck under the Punch and counter
with a Slash to the Hip Flexors.

- Options -

Parry the Punch and counter with a
Slash to the Triceps.

V-Block the Punch and counter
with a Stab then Slash to the
Abdominals.

Parry the Punch and counter with
a Slash to the Chest and Lat.

V-Block the Punch and counter
with a Stab to the Trap.

- Options -

Grab and pin the hand to you and Slash the Wrist Flexors.

Parry the Punch and counter with a Stab to the Trap.

Slip the choke and Slash the Hip Flexors.

Thrust the Knife up into the Throat.

- Options -

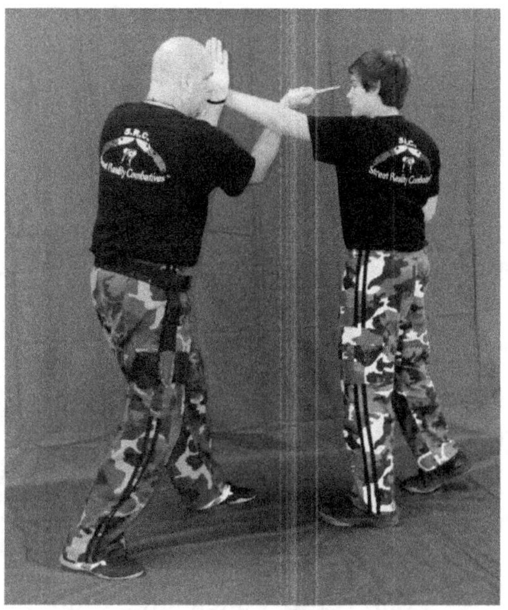

Parry the Punch and Stab the Eye.

V-Block the Punch and Slash the Biceps.

Slip the punch and Slash the Hip Flexors.

Parry the Punch and Slash the Quadriceps.

- Options -

Parry the Grab and Stab the Biceps.

Parry the Punch and Stab the Throat.

Notes:

____

____

____

____

____

____

____

____

____

____

____

____

____

<u>**Notes:**</u>

Training / Seminars

Remember That There is NO Substitute for Personal and Live Training / Instruction.

Books - Videos are good for references only.

Terry Gay is available for:

**- Seminars
- Workshops
- Private Lesson**

**For more Information call:
(616) 364-5111**

www.SuperTKarate.com

E-Mail: supertdojo@gmail.com

B E S A F E

G E T R E A L

9 798458 108423